SOUL

The COSMOLOGY TRILOGY by Joseph Grange

Nature: An Environmental Cosmology (1997)
The City: An Urban Cosmology (1999)
Soul: A Cosmology

SOUL
A Cosmology

JOSEPH GRANGE

Published by State University of New York Press, Albany

© 2011 State University of New York

All rights reserved

Printed in the United States of America

No part of this book may be used or reproduced in any manner whatsoever without written permission. No part of this book may be stored in a retrieval system or transmitted in any form or by any means including electronic, electrostatic, magnetic tape, mechanical, photocopying, recording, or otherwise without the prior permission in writing of the publisher.

For information, contact State University of New York Press, Albany, NY
www.sunypress.edu

Production by Eileen Meehan
Marketing by Anne M. Valentine

Library of Congress Cataloging-in-Publication Data

Grange, Joseph, 1940–
  Soul : a cosmology / Joseph Grange.
      p. cm.
  Includes bibliographical references and index.
  ISBN 978-1-4384-3387-5 (hardcover : alk. paper)
  ISBN 978-1-4384-3388-2 (paperback : alk. paper)
  1. Soul. I. Title.
  BD421.G73 2010
  128'.1—dc22   2010016005

10 9 8 7 6 5 4 3 2 1

For Malachy

Last to arrive

First to turn East

EN UNA NOCHA OSCURA

Con ansias, en amores inflamada
Oh dichosa ventura,
Sali sin ser notada,
Estando ya mi casa sosegada

On a dark night, filled with anxiety
On fire with love
By luck, I got away unnoticed
My house still well guarded
—John of the Cross

[Translated by Hermana Juanita de las Hermanas de San Geronimo, South Bronx, New York]

CONTENTS

Preliminaries	ix
Preface	xi
Introduction	1
1. Inscape	15
2. Involvement	27
3. Feeling the Alternatives	41
4. Eloquence Arising	53
5. Eternal and Temporal Contrasts	69
6. Soul Work	85
7. Signs of the Times	101
Epilogue	117
Postscript	121
Notes	123
Selected Bibliography	135
Index	143

PRELIMINARIES

I begin with the words of John of the Cross for he best describes the flight of the human Soul toward its authentic self-expression. Note the mood, the color, the tone, the feelings, and the setting—obscurity, anxiety, passion, love, chance, security, home—of his words. These are the themes that will accompany us on our journey. It will not be easy because many cultural forces have come upon the scene since John wrote these words in sixteenth-century Spain: brain science, changes in religious forms, alternate interpretations of philosophy, and shifts of vast cultural significance—sexual identity, wars based on religious allegiances, environmental dangers stretching across the planet, global networks of immediate and intense communication, market capitalism on a scale never seen before, political crises with looming threats of thermonuclear attacks—to name but a few.

Two books preceded this one. The first, *Nature: An Environmental Cosmology*, sought to lay out basic categories and structures whereby nature can be understood as a region of value and experience. The second book, *The City: An Urban Cosmology*, sought to do the same for city existence. The major aim of both books was to demonstrate that one could talk normatively about such major dimensions of contemporary life as the natural and the built world. While both volumes can stand on their own, they are interrelated by reason of more than aim. They share a common methodology—the construction of a speculative, systematic cosmology along the lines of that first formulated by Alfred North Whitehead in his *Process and Reality*. As explained in those books cosmology seeks the basic traits of this concrete world and then creates an imaginative hypothetical schema of categories that are then used experimentally to explore the values inherent in the particular circumstances under investigation. Cosmology is not stipulative but rather deeply indebted to imaginative generalizations and their verification through appeal to concrete situations. If successful, the results should give us a deeper appreciation of the values expressed in the activities discussed and, equally important, provide a synoptic view that neither science nor forms of literary expression can provide. In a world such as ours, depth and reach are the primary qualities needed for human intelligence to act positively over a wide range of experiences. Without some such vision we are blind as bats.

In the course of those books I became convinced that one more inquiry was required. At the end of *The City* I wrote: "Like all great philosophical traditions, American philosophy bears witness to the eloquence of the human Soul when it meditates on the mysteries of existence."[1] This cosmological account of the human Soul attempts to redeem the promise latent in those words.

PREFACE

> The eyes are the windows of the soul.

No one knows the origin of this saying, but it is still used even as the most sophisticated brain science continues to develop. A mental health professional is trained to gaze into the eyes of her patient. She is trying to catch sight of a certain look. If the eyes are dead, she is dealing with a very serious mental health problem, possibly some form of schizophrenia. If the eyes are sad, then depression is present. This book is directly concerned with all the elements mentioned in this opening sentence: the eyes are the windows of the Soul. These eyes express feelings and even enduring states of being. How is this so? Is there a Soul? Is the saying declaring that the Soul is "within" the body true? If so, where is it? Is it in the brain, or is it in the mind? But what is mind, and where is it? Questions on questions on questions!

What stands out in this opening scene of client and therapist is the clear understanding that there is some relation between the soul and expression. This book is an exploration of the connection between the Soul and expression. Put most directly, I will be exploring the hypothesis that *the Soul is expression*. The Soul is not the body, nor is it the mind, nor is it the brain. Soul simply is what it is though it has intimate connections with the body, the mind, and the brain. It will take the rest of this book to unravel the meaning and implication of this hypothesis.

My intellectual debts in shaping this project are many. First and foremost is Alfred North Whitehead, who woke me up to the dangers of taking abstractions as real aspects of reality. He called this "The Fallacy of Misplaced Concreteness." He also argued against the "Fallacy of Simple Location," which maintains that isolating particulars is the best way to understand organisms. Whitehead understood that it is the relations between parts that organize the living whole that is an organic event. In understanding this foundational fact he had good company, for it was Spinoza who in the seventeenth century showed that particulars are complex, and wholes are simple. He further argued that this logic of wholes and parts was the only way to overcome the dualism initiated by Descartes earlier in the same century.

The classical American tradition represented by James, Dewey, and Peirce, each in its own way, enabled me to see the dominant power of Soul to be that of the reception of experience and its consequent concrete expression. Further, the tradition of classical American philosophy also showed me that our personal and social worlds are built up from that primordial level of feelings. Contemporary thinkers such as Robert Neville, George Allan, David Weismann, Roger Ames, and the late David Hall have helped me water these intellectual roots. Process philosophers such as John Cobb and David Ray Griffin have also added range and depth to my reflections. Many others could also be named, but I am content to go back to my philosophical father, Plato, whose method of formulating speculative systematic hypotheses so as to discern the value of events made me see the ultimate importance of philosophy as a cultural tool.

In what follows I have tried to be clear without simplifying complex questions. I have also not shied away from questions that are not very popular in contemporary philosophy. I will speak of mystical experience, alternate states of consciousness, God, eternity, and the shifting of temporal experiences within certain settings, such as meditation, art, and prayer. I ask the reader to be patient and to indulge my sense that the recovery of Soul is among the most important tasks of our age.

Without a living concept of Soul, ethics and especially the virtues of honesty and transparency are easily turned into their false opposites—spin, sophistry, the devious use of logic and language, and the continual practice of the high arts of deception. These are not just the results of the Bush administration. They have been going on for a long, long time. As the Rabbi wisely remarked, "The fish always stinks from the head down."

INTRODUCTION

> You could not find out the boundaries of soul, even by traveling along every path: so deep is its expression.
>
> —Heraclitus, Kirk and Raven, *The Presocratic Philosophers*

They called Heraclitus "the Obscure" and "the Dark One." Reading the extant fragments, one can sense how he could easily be given such a designation. But the lines quoted above (my translation)[1] are neither dark nor obscure. They strike me as a celebration of Soul and an open invitation to follow the path of Soul as it expresses itself. What I propose in this study is to take up that invitation and concentrate on Heraclitus's suggestion that Soul is constituted by its expression; he calls it *"Logos."*

RECLAMATION OF SOUL

We begin with a brief look at the history of Soul. The earliest recorded speculations about Soul go as far back as Hindu literature and Greek philosophy. Going further back we find burial rites pointing toward beliefs in another dimension within which Soul may exist. Moving up to the present era we have the continuing debates on the relation between the brain and the mind, which is a variant of the older question of the relations among the body, the mind, and the Soul.

Some seventy-five years ago Whitehead summed up the results of what he called "the Century of Genius" (the seventeenth century) by asserting that the human race was stymied since it had committed itself to a way of thinking it could neither live without nor live with.[2] The ideas in question are the revolution brought about by the division of reality into material and mental domains. This scientific dualism quickly won cultural assent, and ever since we humans have been arguing about how to put Humpty Dumpty together again.[3]

2 / Soul

The slightest survey of the literature involved in the contemporary practice of the philosophy of mind proves the truth of Whitehead's observation. It is a jungle in there. From the materialist perspective one can count more than a dozen proposed solutions. From the idealist point of view one can find a similar number. One can find dualists who choose both sides just as one can find functionalists, computationalists, and behaviorists who ignore both sides. As I read through these approaches, I was reminded of the days before Copernicus when epicycles upon epicycles (read distinctions) were drawn to justify the validity of the Ptolemaic universe.

Turning to the East and its most ancient writings, matters become even more full of twists and turns. The Vedas and Upanishads of Hindu culture speak of a Soul identical with the Ultimate. *Atman* is *Brahman*. Here all is suffering but only because we do not know who we are. Ignorance is to be burned away. What stands unveiled is the Eternal that we actually are. Then Buddhism turns everything upside down by maintaining that there is no such thing as a Soul. There is only *anatta*, no Soul. Moving further east we encounter Taoist and Confucian interpretations that center the Soul in the heart-mind (*xin*) and thereby integrate feeling and thought within a unified field of experience. Cosmos, heaven, earth, and human beings form a field of interdependent relations such that integration in the cosmos is what brings good fortune. Buddhism finds a well-tilled soil as it adapts its doctrine to Chinese culture and earns the designation Ch'an. Finally, Ch'an Buddhism jumps across the Sea of Japan and becomes Zen. The story reaches its present moment when Zen lands in America at the very moment that the sixties witness a massive experiment with drugs by youth, New Age practices proliferate, and brain science helps millions deal with mental health problems.

This brief summary of the cultural forms of Soul suggests that what is at the heart of Soul experience (either as positive or negative) is the active presence of desire. Attachment and clinging are seen as prime movers of the Soul's fortunes. This is especially true of the East. Be it the source of illusion as described in Advaita Vedanta, or when properly reformed, the origin of good karma as in the Bhagavad Gita, desire is the road leading to a true understanding of the workings of Soul. Similarly, even though it rejects the reality of the personal Soul, Buddhism centers its practice on the role of desire in creating worldviews and personal identities.

On the other hand, when we turn to the West we find a stress on the rational dimensions of Soul. From Plato and Aristotle through Descartes, Kant, and Hegel, it is the thinking dimension of Soul that takes center stage, although Plato, Aristotle, Spinoza, and Hegel also recognize the important place of concrete feelings of desire. Similarly, that great empiricist David Hume locates ethical life in the realm of the passions.

But even these generalities break down as we move into the present age. Depth psychology weaves both the affective and the rational together and adds a new dimension, the unconscious. Various schools of social psychology emphasize the formative presence of communal influences within the structures of the Soul. There is therefore a rich and deeply profound culture of the Soul lying all about us. The question is what to do with it. Or put in more traditional language, the ancient and fundamental question of how we shall live still haunts the present age.

I shall argue in this book that the Soul is an act of expression that reveals the creativity lying within the womb of reality. Soul is at its most real when it can creatively integrate its various dimensions of desire, feeling, will, and reason. The basic function of the Soul (even in those cultures that deny its ultimate reality) is to bring together the factions that compete for our attention and drive our forms of action. Are we by nature destined for conflicted lives? Or is there a way to unify ourselves and live wholehearted lives? The aim of this study is to provide an understanding of the Soul that can carry us forward toward a balanced mode of existence. I realize this is no small undertaking, but philosophy's duty has always been to face up to such ultimate challenges.

Much more will later be said about these themes. For now I wish to underline four central points that are indispensable for an understanding of this study:

1. The Soul is an activity and is not to be thought of as a thing.
2. The activity of the Soul is the transformation of itself and its environment.
3. This transformation is always an act of expression.
4. The transformative action of the Soul involves the creative integration of ever-changing modes of togetherness.

The first point means that one does not *have* a Soul but rather one *is* a Soul. The second point tells us that Souls grow, develop, and can also decay. The third point is crucial for understanding how the Soul actually works. It does so through creative expression. The fourth point identifies the central expressive activity of the Soul: *forging relations that imaginatively integrate its experience.*

Activity means that something is happening. This also implies time, for time is the happening of a difference. This difference is the creative novelty brought into the world by the events that populate it. But there is more to Soul activity than time. There is also the eternal. In this study time and eternity are not to be thought of as two separate realms but rather as distinctly different dimensions of one reality. It will take effort and patience to develop and argue this point. Our culture is not at all friendly to talk about eternity. Another aspect of this study that will require serious effort is the possibility of direct experiences of reality. Such a possibility involves a phenomenology of consciousness initiated by William James and carried to completion by Alfred North Whitehead. One aspect of this direct experience is the reassertion of the central importance of subjectivity in the methodology of neurobiology. This factor introduces the reality of the invisible as an essential ingredient in Soul work. It is at this point that the question of the possibility of human contact with eternity becomes relevant. Here is the point of intersection between the visible and the invisible, or as it is more commonly expressed the empirical and the rational. It is within this interdependence of eternal and temporal connection with the real that the eloquence of Soul most powerfully expresses itself. And for the most part and most paradoxically, this expression is silence. Another expression for this dimension of my study is the *spiritual domain*. How do we make intellectually responsible as well as culturally available such concepts as eternity and the spiritual? They are, to be sure, major dimensions of the story of Soul. They once were vivid parts of human culture, but they have by now receded into the background of what we consider important. Restoring their significance is a major goal of this study.

As mentioned in the preface I have written two previous books that use the philosophical method called "cosmology." Both *Nature: An Environmental Cosmology* (1997) and *City: An Urban Cosmology* (1999) leaned heavily on this methodology. It has a long and distinguished history, though, like Soul itself, it also has suffered from neglect. Most if not all of Hindu, Chinese, and Buddhist philosophy is cosmological. In the West, Plato and Aristotle, Aquinas and Scotus, Descartes, Spinoza and Leibniz, Kant and Hegel, and in American philosophy Peirce, Whitehead, and Dewey were practitioners of this art. To expand on my prefatory remarks, cosmology seeks to structure well-crafted hypotheses about the subject matter to be discussed. It is therefore not stipulative but hypothetical. Furthermore it demands that these hypotheses be logically consistent and testable in real experience. Therefore, cosmology has two sides. It is systematic and speculative in the sense that it seeks to select out and then order the important traits of the experience to be examined. This is its rational side. But it is also empirical for it demands that its hypothesis be tested in real experience and yield important results.

The benefits of cosmology are threefold. First, it is honest for it lays all its cards on the table right at the beginning. Second, this method should result in a synoptic vision that ties together diverse regions of experience and value. This power to connect ideas and events is not driven by the "totalizing will to power" condemned by Heidegger and other postmodern thinkers. Rather it has the distinctly positive goal of trying, as best as one can, *not* to leave anything out. Its perspectives must be inclusive enough to do justice to all forms of experience. The cosmological method is not hegemonic, but necessarily generous and open; otherwise, it is just bad cosmology. If done adequately, this study should integrate the environment (Nature), culture (The City), and spiritual (Soul). Third, this method also has its empirical side. When employed to understand experience, it should display new connections and surprising relations and spur on thought to deepen and widen its efforts to understand and experience reality. Finally, in keeping with American philosophy's experimental spirit, cosmology always acknowledges its fallibility and is ready to change its findings when reason and experience demand such correction.

Foremost among the ideas brought forth by this cosmology is the concept of Soul (and everything else in the universe) as an *Expression*. On the surface this may seem to be not much of an idea, but when systematically presented and advanced in a creative manner, it can transform our understanding of the way in which we experience and comprehend reality. What is it that reality is all about? What happens when something comes to be? What are the underlying connections that bind reality together? The answer to each question is expression. Now expression means manifestation of a special kind. It signifies the emergence into being of *that which has not been before*. Expression names the coming-to-be of novelty. Expression is the creative dynamic driving the universe forward. Expression never stops. It is ceaseless in its striving to come into being. It is what makes every being be. It is the desire that haunts the human spirit. *Expression is the sign made when something happens.*

It will be noticed that in the course of writing this introduction I have dropped the definite article when speaking of Soul. This is deliberate. To speak of "the Soul" is to raise a host of problems that are not germane to this study. In the first place, "the Soul" inevitably brings to mind a substance and not what the Soul actually is: *a process or event ever in development by reason of its relations.* "The" also emphasizes the subject predicate language that is a major obstacle in communicating my understanding of Soul. To repeat what I said before: Soul is not a thing but a stretch of experience that can grow, become static, or decay. This is to say (with Whitehead) "that how an actual entity comes to be constitutes what that actual entity is."[4] We are not first a substance that acquires and then exhibits qualities. We are first an event that expresses its way of becoming through the quality of its actions. *How we become is what we are.* This is the foundation of my thesis that expression is the meaning of Soul. Also, later in this book, I will be speaking of "Soul making." Expressions such as "*the* Soul works" or "*the* Soul desires" or "*the* Soul can mistake" are not lucid enough to convey the meaning I intend. At first, the word *Soul* may seem odd, awkward, or even inept. One measure of my success in discussing Soul ought to be greater ease in using this ancient word. To sum up I shall argue that Soul is an act of expression that reveals the creativity lying within the womb of reality. Soul is at its most real when it can integrate its various dimensions of desire, feeling, will, and reason and express that integration in an eloquent way.

What about the vexed question of the connections, if any, among body, matter, brain and mind, consciousness, or Soul? I shall argue that Soul is neither body nor mind. It is rather the concreteness that is both source and outcome of the abstraction called "body" and the abstraction called "mind." Gilbert Ryle was only half right when he spoke of "the ghost in the machine." We are the victims of a category mistake, but the mistake lies in using an inadequate category to try to capture the reality of Soul. Soul is an organic process. Its reality resides in its power to integrate the various dimensions of human existence. The measure of its value is the quality of the connections it is able to forge and communicate. Arguing this thesis is the essence of my study. I call this activity of binding the various dimensions of experience "Expression."

Finally, this book could not have been written if not for David Ray Griffin's masterful *Unsnarling the World Knot.* My commitment to Whitehead's philosophic vision is obvious and Professor Griffin has used that same vision to confront and argue against the major positions of those scholars actively working in the discipline of the philosophy of mind. My project is the reconstruction and restoration of Soul to its proper place in human culture. It differs from his, but he has demonstrated that a conceptual breakthrough is required if our culture is to break the logjam infecting the philosophy of mind. I take his arguments as convincing and use them as a platform for my own efforts regarding the human Soul. I express my gratitude and request readers to consult his work if certain issues in this work appear to be given short shrift.[5]

It is vital that flesh, bone, suffering, and agony become part of this study. I offer the following that was part of a Ken Burns documentary on the days of slavery. "We stand at the edge of a cotton field. One must be very quiet and make no movement. It is difficult to hear but if you listen keenly, there comes a faint noise that sounds like an owl's 'hoot.' It is a human sound and it comes from the slaves recently arrived from Africa and quickly bought up by the owner at the latest auction. It may very well be their first time in the slave fields. They are communicating with one another. It cannot be understood by the slave driver or by us. It is a whisper and at the same time an expression and it *is* there."[6]

It is there in all its beauty and in all its terror—an almost soundless expression of pain and the longing for support and company. Someone needs to be recognized by someone else. We will never know what the message carried, but it was, is, and will forever be *an act of expression*. It is this act of expression that forms the heart of this study of Soul.

Clues to the meaning of this act of expression are scattered throughout Eastern and Western philosophy. The Upanishad says: *Tat tvam asi*. The Daodejing says Ziran and Dao. The Buddha is called "Tathagata." Parmenides speaks of the One that expresses everything and yet remains one. There is also the saying of Heraclitus cited earlier. Plato in the Seventh Letter speaks of a spark that flies between teacher and student and then "kindles itself." Aristotle tells us that in its act of knowing, Soul in a way can become all things. Spinoza uses logic to unfold the unity that Soul is capable of experiencing in the multiplicity of the universe. Hegel expresses the object of his search as *die Sache Selbst* and then paradoxically finds it expressed in diverse limited forms of consciousness. Finally in our age Bergson speaks as follows:

> The farther we go, the more terms we discover; we shall never say all that could be said, and yet, if we turn back suddenly upon the impulse that we feel behind us, and try
>
> to seize it, it is gone; for *it was not a thing but the direction of a movement*, and though indefinitely extensible, it is infinitely simple.[7]

And to conclude, Alfred North Whitehead speaks of a truthful beauty that expresses the creative processes that lie beyond verbal expression.

Expression in its various forms has been a key to the evolution of all biological species. Signs, sounds, gestures, symbols, and words are critical. It is the presence of signs that announces the arrival of life in its seemingly infinite variety. With signs come meanings and the possibility of new perspectives that may yield further understanding. All this connects with the words, "In the beginning was the word."[8] From grunts to songs, from scratchings to paintings, from wandering to finding the way—these deeply felt human experiences rest upon the power of expression.

Even today Soul still expresses some of the most living human experiences as in 'Soul' music, 'Soul' food, and "Soul" brother and "Soul" sister. The cunning of history has made "Soul" the cultural property of those who were originally dispossessed of life. The journey from whispers in a slave field to the explosive power of "the Soul Man," James Brown, is testimony of the power of life still expressing itself in Soul.

Soul is a now a dead word. How ironic! For ages it had been used to signify the presence of life, and now it lies before us empty of meaning. True enough, human beings still use it for religious purposes and spiritual movements speak of it as real. But the big movers and shakers of our culture would rather be caught dead than utter it in a serious assembly. The professor who uses it risks ridicule. Still, the word hangs on and often receives wistful expression in the conversations of today's college students. When there is something in the air—think of the sixties or Vietnam or civil rights marches or for that matter any of the still-to-be-defined human cultural movements—it is the unexpressed presence of Soul that calls for expression.

Life and death dance around expressions of Soul. Soul was once used to mark off the living from the dead. Today it is replaced by such terms as *self* or *person* and has ceased to be a matter of discussion in our public institutions. Soul is now confined to religious and spiritual domains. The results of this quarantine can be seen in the increasing thinness of the concept and the consequent loss of a significant human dimension. This study seeks to recover its living meaning for our time. To listen to the slave hoot is to hear the call of Soul.

PLAN OF THIS STUDY

This effort to retrieve Soul as a most important dimension of human culture is best viewed as a pilgrimage toward an experience all but forgotten in our time. I have tried to capture the force of this ascending journey of expression in the title of the fourth chapter—Eloquence Arising. The pathway toward Soul as expression begins with a detailed exposition of the foundational features of Soul. This is the goal of the first three chapters. It then reaches a plateau in chapters 4 and 5 where the connections among expression, the temporal world, and eternity are spelled out. From this vantage point the work required to anchor Soul as a living, habitual force in contemporary life and culture can be seen, felt, and understood.

My method follows the path laid out in the first two books of this trilogy. As previously explained, I follow the cosmological method laid out by Plato, Confucius, Aristotle, Spinoza, Hegel, and Whitehead and others in both the Eastern and Western philosophical traditions in seeking to evoke the generic traits of Soul. I then attempt to describe systematically how these features connect with each other. I intend to paint an intensely real portrait. This allusion to aesthetics is deliberate, for my use of reason leans heavily on the Chinese method of stressing the ways in which the particulars of experience create their own orders without relying on a preordained order. The whole emerges from a trust in the particulars as they manifest their significantly different values. In *Modes of Thought* Whitehead says: "The distinction between logic and aesthetics consists in the degree of abstraction involved. Logic concentrates attention on high abstraction, and aesthetics keeps as close to the concrete as the necessities of finite understanding allow. Thus logic and aesthetics are two extremes of the dilemma of the finite mentality in its partial penetration of the infinite."[9] In this study I call this kind of reasoning "felt intelligence," a term defined and extensively used in my other books. In the beginning this may cause difficulty because we are not at all accustomed to bringing together feeling and thinking. But that is exactly what the Chinese, as stated above, do when they call their thinking organ *"xin,"* which is best translated as "HeartMind." This is also what lies behind my frequent use of such terms as *Contrast* and *Harmony*. They are concepts that must be felt and thought for their full force to be grasped by human consciousness. As this pilgrimage moves toward the eternal and the spiritual, it will depend more and more on our willingness to explore felt intelligence as the most direct means to experience Soul.

But I do not throw the logical dimension to the winds. This can be shown by an examination of the central points of each chapter and how they relate to each other.

Chapter 1, "Inscape," sketches a hypothesis to be employed and tested in the rest of our study. It maintains that there are certain definable features of Soul. Among these are subjectivity, intensity of feeling, creativity, integration, transformation, and personal unity. Expression integrates human expression. It can even move Soul from the dull ache of confusion to the brilliance of eloquence arising. What I call "the factor of the integer" makes possible the fusion of the affective and rational dimensions of Soul. This concept is derived from what Susanne Langer in her masterpiece *Mind: An Essay on Human Feeling* calls the importance of 'the Act' in the gestation of the human mind as an organ based on feeling.[10] The chapter concludes with the advent of active reason that rises up from ever deepening levels of intensity. It is this felt intelligence that will escort us through the rest of the pilgrimage.

Chapter 2, "Involvement," introduces the social dimension of Soul's activity. It argues for the need to communicate in order fully to grasp the extensive reach of expression. Doing and Knowing become interlocked as essential dimensions of felt intelligence. The edges of egotism that threatened to choke Soul in the previous chapter are softened by the need to recognize others. Ego reduction will become a significant aspect of Soul's growth as it continues to develop its full expressive powers. This fusion of action, feeling, and thinking, as expressed in Rilke's "Panther"—"An image enters it, /rushes down through the tense arrested muscles,/plunges into the heart and is gone"—brings this study to the next chapter's discussion of consciousness.

Chapter 3, "Feeling the Alternatives," offers a realistic understanding of consciousness based on Whitehead's succinct description of this experience as "the affirmation of a negation." Consciousness is Soul expressing itself at a new level. When a sense of the alternative is felt, then Soul recognizes how different approaches to situations can be of enormous help in broadening personal and social cohesion. It is here that the fundamental features of Soul find their final integration, and the possibility of genuine creative transformation expresses itself. It is also the moment when truth becomes important for consciousness introduces the quality of "Appearance" into human life and culture. "Spin" may be as likely as direct truth, so ethics becomes vital for the expression of Soul truth. As Soul becomes aware of itself, others, and, in some way the whole, a Rubicon has been crossed. Now contrast and harmony come into play. Soul must begin to explore effective ways to find more and more difference to widen its previous self-absorption. The meaning of beauty as an ultimate measure for judging the varying values gained by sheltering differences under identity begins to express itself. At this point the expression of meaning becomes a spiritual act. Poise is the virtue most needed by Soul as it strives to express an arising eloquence in the presence of so much difference. Chapters 1, 2, and 3 have laid the groundwork for integrating inscape, social interaction, and consciousness. The task of articulating eloquence and its relation to spirituality has arrived.

Chapters 4 and 5 establish a plateau from which Soul's destiny and powers can at the very least be glimpsed if not directly experienced. They are also the most abstract and difficult chapters in this study; nevertheless, their subject matters are crucial for continuing on the road of eloquence.

Chapter 4, "Eloquence Arising," uses the semiotic metaphysics of Charles Sanders Peirce and Whitehead's theory of "Truthful Beauty." Peirce understood Soul to be a sign, and like all signs it has to traverse the difficult circumstances of firstness, secondness, and thirdness. Firstness expresses itself as an icon that is fresh, spontaneous, and novel. It engages us and grabs our attention. It is a special favorite of our culture because it helps fasten Soul to a single-minded point of view. Icons, however, are always tested by secondness for what is new must meet the challenges of what is already established. The expression of secondness is the index—that which tests the reality of an icon. If an index demonstrates the failed reality of an icon, then that moment of engagement is dead. It cannot survive the push and pull of actual existence. Let us suppose that icon and index are in synchronic rhythm. $1 + 2 = 3$. Thirdness is the maturation of a sign. It may also be called a "symbol." It is the acme of eloquence, for on the one hand it has proved itself, and on the other hand the community has also accepted it as a lasting and arresting expression of what is concretely real. Through such expressions Soul achieves stable places of genuine stature in the life of a community. How long this sign will remain eloquently recognizable depends on its strength and the situations it will face. If it has authentic depth, then new dimensions of meanings will express themselves in the continuing history of the community. If it is shallow and sterile, it will merely degenerate into an entertaining diversion or an inconsequential fact. Our culture has an alarming lack of rich, compelling symbols that can express the many unions of identity and difference that make up a thriving community. It lives on the thin gruel of depleted signs that give birth to an entertained society, or it degenerates into a series of clichés whose meaning has lost all affective power. It is no wonder that 'Soul' is a dead word.

"Truthful Beauty" is Whitehead's eloquent symbol for that mode of expression that brings together identity and difference so that a fusion of opposites explodes with meaning. It demands exceptional imaginative power that can bring into existence novel forms of meaning that lie beyond the dictionary meaning of words. This nonverbal experience culminates in eloquent expression. At this level of expression beauty's harmonic power is made direct, robust, stalwart, and strong by the presence of truth. There is no perfume of empty suggestiveness, nor are there sly, deceptive manifestations of the unreal. What is now there has not been there before, and it is indelible in its eloquence and unforgettable in its expression. Eloquent signs are the lifeblood of Soul. Eloquence is that which achieves the most with the least, and when it arises, it is the sign of a poised culture unafraid to express its values.

Chapter 5, "Eternal and Temporal Contrasts" provides a stunning vision of what is possible for Soul if it can grasp the dynamic relations between time and eternity. This is the most abstract chapter, but the rewards for understanding this theme through felt intelligence lead directly to certain contemporary spiritual and therapeutic practices. The potential of this dialectic to transform Soul's present poverty into the richest realms of expressive meaning provides realistic hope that our culture can reclaim Soul as a living personal reality. I rely on the works of Robert Neville and Spinoza to provide an introduction to certain ideas about feeling and knowing the dynamics of eternity and time. The three modes of time—the past, the present, and the future—are not self-explanatory because no one of them can explain the existence of the other two. Therefore, unless one wishes to accept an irrational world (existentialists do this and so do certain Vedanta philosophers), one must postulate an eternal realm within which the modes of time are established by divine creativity. *But there is no time in eternity.* Thus time and eternity constitute one subject and not two. *Time does flow* because God through a singular act has eternally set the modes of time. Bringing both time and eternity together has been the desire of those humans who all over this planet and during all epochs of civilization have struggled first to experience such a dynamic and second to find ways to express it. The life of Eternity is the life of God in which to some degree humans can share. History testifies to the extraordinary fact that Souls in the past and in the present have taken on the task of walking this road.

To fuse together the realms of Being and Becoming is the most intense experience Soul can have. The possibility of such an experience is real, and many human Souls have claimed to have had such moments. It would not be intellectually responsible to dismiss such experiences. The variety of methods used to feel intelligently such moments are understandably numerous and still available. The remaining chapters of this study are given over to exploring two distinctive ways and means to make concrete such possibilities.

Chapter 6, "Soul Making," steers Soul's pilgrimage in the direction of action. It suggests a program of meditative action that can move Soul toward a finite but intelligible feel for the eternal/temporal dialectic. Such an orientation can break the vapid neurotic circularity that infects contemporary Soul. The unity of action and knowing is the outcome of felt alternatives arising from the depths of consciousness. As the great Neo-Confucian philosopher Wang Yang-ming (d. 1529) maintained, "Those who know and do not act do not know."[11]

I once again take up the vision of Spinoza for he draws a concrete picture of how this union of thought and action can be put to work for the benefit of Soul. In providing a compelling logical and emotional analysis of Soul's power to unite the temporal and eternal dynamic, he points the way toward the making of an eloquent Soul. He argues that there is only one really real being of which we are finite modes. This being Spinoza calls "God," "Nature," or "Substance." It is self-creative, eternal, necessary, and infinite. I follow Neal Grossman who in his magnificent book *Healing the Mind* names it with simple eloquence: "**ALL-THERE-IS**."[12] Spinoza maintains that our chief enslavement is caused by our emotional life that can either drive us away from **ALL-THERE-IS** or bring us closer to its power. We have the ability to know reality through what Spinoza calls "*scientia intuitiva*." This highest form of knowledge allows us to begin to understand things as **ALL-THERE-IS** knows them. Such knowledge diminishes our negative emotions and prompts us to enjoy life with greater energy, strength, and self-esteem. Our life can culminate in what Spinoza calls the "the Intellectual Love of God."

This is the supreme fusion of felt intelligence with the eternally necessary and utterly creative order of ALL-THERE-IS and is marked by our sense of identity with that order. We, too, have a part of our mind that is eternal, and this understanding love and/or loving understanding is the source of our supreme happiness. A fairy tale? Perhaps, but I will provide a reading of the *Ethics* that challenges such a claim. Spinoza's analysis of our emotions and their power is compelling, and his claim that we too have an eternal dimension to our thinking is a vital element of authentic Soul work. Spinoza offers us an opportunity to lead an active life unchained from the negative emotions that sap our personal and cultural attitude.

Chapter 7, "Signs of the Times," closes this study with an examination of our present cultural situation. I maintain that a new "Battle of the Giants" now stalks the land. Contemporary Soul is caught between two signs: *the sign of diversion* and *the sign of mindfulness*. The former, Diversion, seeks to divert us from what is important through the many forms of our cultural malaise and dysfunction. The other, Mindfulness, is the outcome of a spiritual and therapeutic practice that is often called "meditation" or "contemplation" (many other terms can also be used). I offer it as a living alternative to its sworn enemy Diversion. I present this other way of living through the Soul work of two contemporary persons, Bhante Gunaratana Henepola, a Theravada Buddhist Monk who advocates Vipassana meditation, and Aaron Beck, the founder of the psychotherapeutic school of cognitive therapy (CT). Both persons discuss and employ all that has been said about reason in this study—felt intelligence, active reason, aesthetic reason and logical reason—and as these concepts receive concrete expression in their Soul work, the full speech of Soul at work comes to the fore. If a Buddhist practice, Vipassana, and a secular discipline, CT, can join hands in dealing with the sense of overwhelming pressures that crushes the lives of so many, then we can see how mindfulness can function as a bridge between psychotherapy and spirituality. Philosophy as the love of wisdom can reclaim its proper place among the important cultural disciplines of our time. To conclude, I quote Hegel who devoted a lifetime of effort to grasping the links between spirit and reason: "[L]anguage is the Soul existing as Soul."[13]

Soul ends with an epilogue that offer a *repris* of all these themes from the perspective of wisdom understood as knowing the ways in which fact and value intersect to support each other. Such wisdom is what philosophy has in its best moments always sought.

1

INSCAPE

> Each mortal thing does one thing and the same: . . . Crying *What I do is me: for that I came.*
>
> —Gerard Manley Hopkins, "As Kingfishers Catch Fire, Dragonflies Draw Flame"

Any process of growth must sink its roots into deep, rich soil. This chapter struggles to uncover those roots. This first approach to Soul involves describing insofar as it is possible its character and functions. I call this the task of "painting the inscape of Soul." As explained in *Nature* and *The City*, the term *inscape* is borrowed from the work of the great Jesuit poet Gerard Manley Hopkins.[1] Devoted to the insistent particularity of all the events of the cosmos, Hopkins used this term to identify the great effort needed to express on the outside what is going on in the inside. A particular fact of creation expresses itself when individuality is woven in, on, and through the web of connections within which it is born. This rise into being is marked by the expression of degrees of intensity. Poets have long recognized the value of each and every such act of expression. John Keats spoke of human life as "a vale of soul making," and Aristotle spoke of living things as having Souls. In the course of history the Greek word *psyche* becomes the Latin *anima*. Thenceforth we speak of animation as the very sign of life itself.[2] *Anima* is expression itself. Hopkins found deep resonances in the philosophy of Duns Scotus who regarded divine creativity as an act of will that was to be understood as God's eros driving into the cosmos itself and thereby releasing myriad forms of individual creativity. He called each of these instances of creative expression in the Latin a *"haecceitas" w*hich literally translated means "thisness." *What is,* is *what it expresses itself to be.* At this primordial level of being, one is reduced to speaking like a child; however, this is where the roots of expression are to be found. God, for Scotus, creates through eros and wills maximum individuality. Strength of individuality is an instance of creative force that brings difference into the world.

It would be difficult to exaggerate the importance of uniqueness for this study of Soul. It will emerge again and again as the subject of expression expands. The history of human reflection—East and West—testifies to its continuing importance. Suchness, *Tathagata, Tat Tvam Asi, Dao, Ziran* in Asia; *To Hen, Logos, Eidos, Ousia, Substantia,* Monads, *die Sache Selbst,* actual occasions, and experience in the West. Each concept amplifies and deepens the expression of what in itself is inexpressible—the absolute uniqueness of each Soul.

Contemporary society, even in its most intense postmodern forms, is still reacting to two aspects of the Enlightenment: expression and autonomy.[3] In this sense my proposed change in understanding Soul is in line with today's insistence upon the significance of language and the connections between subjectivity and freedom. I know that the uses to which I put these concepts will not satisfy many postmodern thinkers. But no one has a license to define what is reasonable, especially since postmodern thinkers have consistently courted "unreason" and limited the use of freedom despite freedom's very meaning.

In considering Soul as the expression of experienced freedom, I am following a formidable tradition whose lineage includes distinguished medieval thinkers. Great Renaissance artists have also lent their power to this way of understanding. And of course, the emergence of the subjective realm is the signature of the modern age. In our own day, the neurosciences have entered so powerfully into the discussion that it is unthinkable to ignore the fact that the expression and the freedom that make up the inscape of Soul are carried out by an embodied subject. The fact is that the body, and most especially the brain, is a major contributing element that both enables and limits Soul's expressive capacities. There is also the social body of the cultural community whose demands and supports are necessary for Soul to express its creative efforts. Finally, evolution and human history are part and parcel of any study of Soul.

I begin by suggesting certain dimensions of the inscape of Soul:

Subjectivity
Intensity of feeling
Creativity
Integration and Transformation
Personal Unity

Each of these features results from what Hopkins called the "instress" that inhabits individuals. Instress is the activity expressed by Soul's features. Instress and inscape are ways of understanding *form* as an active agent in a world of becoming. Form is not a lifeless idea best buried alongside Plato. A form is a limit, and the limits imposed on process make up the determinations that make a creature a definite *this* rather than a *that*. This was captured by Hopkins' eye, ear, and mind as he sought to express the Soul of things. Instress is the poet's insight into the unending process of things—an insight exemplified in a work of genius such as Hopkins' "That Nature Is a Heraclitean Fire and the Comfort of the Resurrection." Form breathes fire into the universe.

Subjectivity is one part of what materialists call "the hard problem"; another hard part is consciousness itself. The act of being a subject does not show up in the materialists' empirical data. It looks like nothing, has no mass or extension, and cannot be empirically measured. And yet our deepest experiences as Souls tell us emphatically that it is there. It is the source of our psychic joy and our psychic pain. It is what convinces us of the fact that we are persons. It is the ground of our identity. It is the mark of the determinateness that sets the limits of our being in the world. To be a subject is to be the center of the Soul powers under discussion. The modern world begins its rise with the words of Descartes: "[But] what then am I? A thinking thing. And what is that? Something that doubts, understands, affirms, denies, wills, refuses, and also senses and has mental images."[4] Spinoza, Leibniz, and Kant develop this concept in various ways. Some two hundred years after Descartes, Hegel underlines the absolute importance of the term for modern philosophy when he writes in the "Preface" to *The Phenomenology of Spirit* that "everything depends on comprehending and expressing the true not as substance but also equally true as subject."[5] What Hegel means by "subject" is a center of self-organizing power that can in its human form express itself as self-consciousness. It is therefore the living, evolving, and developing spirit that is the Soul in action. There may be much that is problematic in Hegel's philosophy, but his development of Spirit (read Soul) in the *Phenomenology* is an important factor in undertaking a reconstruction of Soul.

Intensity of Feeling as a philosophical idea makes its first systematic appearance in the work of Alfred North Whitehead. It expresses directly and concretely the value attained by the world's creatures. When a certain degree of intensity is reached, consciousness and self-consciousness emerge as real factors in experience. For the most part the material world exhibits a predictable steadiness that expresses itself as the laws of nature. Life shifts the equation and introduces what Whitehead calls a "bid for freedom." Higher level animals and human beings mark their arrival by the act of expressing conscious reactions to their environments and their own states of being.[6] Finally, when language develops another stage in expression is reached. Whitehead writes: "The account of the last day of creation should be rewritten, He gave them speech, and they became souls."[7] Intensity is to be judged by its quality and not its quantity. Creativity is most evident when degrees of intensity are increased.

The onset of *Creativity* is also the emergence of difference. When difference happens, time emerges. Professor Guy Debrock has formulated three elementary propositions that sum up creativity at work in a world of process:

1. Nothing is until something happens.
2. Nothing happens unless it involves interaction.
3. Nothing happens in isolation.[8]

Creativity can be as slight as the movement from one moment of time to another—what was now is. It can also be as complex as the interactions of brain components at work when thresholds of consciousness are reached. Creativity signifies that a boundary has been crossed and a new line drawn. Novelty is the outcome of genuine creativity. This primordial originality distinguishes all creatures and is direct evidence of Soul at work. There is in Soul an element of *causa sui* that is the ground of freedom. A natural spontaneity is part of Soul's sway. In human beings the degree of creativity is proportional to the presence of Soul and this self-command is the root of basic individuality—the *Haecceitas* that Duns Scotus and Hopkins insisted was the very inscape of Soul. Call it "freshness" or call it "Dao," it is what has struck Asian, European, and American cultures when Soul is experienced directly.[9] Without creativity there would be nothing for Soul to express and without expression there is no creativity on display. Although not limited to art, creativity finds rich, strong, and commanding presence within aesthetic experience. In many ways art is the royal road to the character of Soul as expression. Art provides significant measures for estimating the value of creativity in the sweep of human culture. But there is more to creativity: when experienced as the sense of an alternative (which we will see is the meaning of consciousness), it gives birth to a real force in the world. Creativity is the original energy underlying expressions such as Gandhi's Soul force (*satyagraha*). Its absence is remarked when we speak of events as Soulless. And finally in metaphysical terms, creativity is the heart of a process universe. Creativity works its magic through involved interaction. It establishes community where once there was emptiness.

Integration and Transformation: this dimension of the inscape of Soul finds expression everywhere life has appeared. On the human level one of its most forceful expressions is to be found in what is called the "Big Book" of Alcoholics Anonymous. Having described the steps required for transformation, it declares: "Many of us exclaimed, 'What an order, I can't go through with it!' Do not be discouraged. No one among us has been able to attain anything like perfect adherence to these principles. We are not saints. The point is, that we are willing to grow along spiritual lines. The Principles we have set down are guides to progress. We claim spiritual progress rather than spiritual perfection."[10]

It is mostly here in the sphere of self-transformation that the spiritual dimension of the human person expresses itself. There are situations where material elements are needed to restore balance to the human body. There are also situations were the human mind needs reconstruction in terms of its reasoning processes. Later in this study Spinoza will be of great help in understanding how these seemingly different aspects work together through their inherent identity. When it comes to integrating the whole person—body and mind—it is the work of Soul that establishes the wholeness of the human person. Psychotherapists know this when they speak of the need for the patient to act as the ultimate factor of integration in their growth toward health. I call this act "spiritual" for a number of reasons. Much of this study is given over to exploring and arguing for the reality of the spiritual realm as an authentic human dimension. But here at the very start an essential aspect of human experience needs emphatic underlining. I call it "the expression of Soul work." Robert Neville has defined Soul in this way: "A self or soul consists of a person's engagement with realities, ultimate and otherwise, and its structures have to do with how the person is oriented with reference to the realities and integrates the different structures of orientation."[11] This description of Soul brings together issues that our culture continues to struggle with: Soul, person, self, will, perspectives, and structures of orientation. In many ways this definition fits better with an Asian view of the human existence rather than a Western one. The idea of integration of one's self and situation strikes many Western ears as a foreign and impossible wish. Asian cultures—Hindu, Buddhists, Confucian, and Taoist—are much more comfortable with this integrative vision. However, one could find similar descriptions of Soul in Jewish, Christian, and Islamic cultures.

Engagements, orientations, perspectives, and structures of engagements are the elements that most concern us in this attempt to recapture the elusive nature of "Soul." Its bewildering dimensions are due to the failed nature of the categories employed to express Soul. At the beginning it is best to keep the understanding of Soul as open and wide as possible. If that is not done, the possibility of marginalizing some of its major dimensions is very real. Neville's definition has the advantage of bringing into the discussion reality ("ultimate or otherwise"), the self, the person, engagements, orientations, and perspectives. At the very least this definition shows the astounding width of Soul's inscape.

The weakening of integrative powers eventually drives human culture into the extreme dualisms that confound contemporary discussions of brain, mind, and Soul. What does it mean to integrate? At its basic metaphysical level this is the classic problem of the one and the many. But the act of integration also involves growth, normative thinking, and command of different types of order as well as sensitivity to the history of human culture. At the heart of this Herculean task is what I term the "factor of the integer." When it is present, then the whole is transformed into more than the sum of its parts. When it is absent, expression deteriorates into a heap of sorites.

What renders the factor of the integer so difficult to pin down is that it takes place as an activity. The integer is that which makes a process whole, unified and complete, but it cannot completely end the movement of process for that would violate the very meaning of process. But we are able to speak of "localized authoritative wholes."[12] Whitehead also terms such a moment of achievement "perfection according to its own kind" for it expresses the human Soul's power to attain to levels of excellence within its finite range of personal inscape.[13] The creativity enacted here can be called "eloquence" since it maximizes intensity of value through minimum effort.[14] The power to integrate itself within its situation is the ground of Soul's personal unity.

Personal Unity results from such eloquence and brings the discussion back to the value of particulars as expressed in the depth of their own creative integration. Susanne Langer has made "The Act" the metaphysical cornerstone of her analysis of mind as the process of expressing the feeling derived from asserting one's place in the universe.[15] This can begin with the most insignificant of ontological assertions and culminate in the great works of aesthetic excellence that adorn the universe.[16] The attainment of personal unity is a long journey and its travail involves many issues—from infantile absorption in the mother, through social separation and recognition, to the development of conscience and onwards to personal creative activity and responsibility. My point here is to underline what has already been implied in the foregoing discussion of the results of the Soul's attempt to work out its inscape through the process of instress. Growth and development depend in the first place on the shadowy creation of a self image. This act of imagination is a leading factor in the Soul work of the person. As this image shifts and changes, it leads the person forward toward an increasingly more unified self identity. Soul work conspires with environment to establish a subject capable of organizing its many parts. This activity increases or decreases the intensity of feeling experienced by the subject as it creative powers emerge. As these feelings are integrated and the subject experiences a sense of its own uniqueness (*haecceitas*), the importance of maintaining unity expresses itself. To be a Soul-self is to be a singular one among the many. It is the argument of this book that the success or failure of such an achievement hangs on the quality of the Soul work carried out by the person. In other words our unity as persons depends upon the matchless unity each of us can carve out through our expressions.

It is important to note the dominance of images in the building of personal unity. Indeed without a healthy self-image growth and development are all but impossible. Once again, Susanne Langer's masterpiece is of direct assistance. She insists that brain science cannot answer the kinds of questions that philosophers ask about mind because they work out of a mode of inquiry based upon models. This methodology is anchored in a commitment to strict causal analysis of the real. Such a way of thinking is from the very outset blinded to the presence of feeling as an integral part of Soul's inscape. It can measure material effects based on quantitative changes. The domain of the qualitative, however, does not enter the world of physical science. This is, of course, but one more example of Whitehead's fallacy of misplaced concreteness: the concreteness of mind is misplaced and shuffled off to the quantitative domain where exact measurement can most effectively do its work. Without recourse to imagery the presence of personal unity anchored in intense feeling remains blocked from view.

One must look to the artist for clues as to how mind and nature work in tandem as acts of expression. Consider the fact that in addition to Langer the following philosophers have held a similar position: C. S. Peirce, Iris Murdoch, David Bohm, John Dewey, Alfred North Whitehead, and Merleau-Ponty. Peirce saw esthetics as the ground of logic, metaphysics, and ethics. Langer's great study of feeling and the mind provides a definitive argument for using aesthetic images to get at the subjective reality of mind. Iris Murdoch, as we have seen, uses aesthetics to define the "local authorized wholes" that are the key to valid knowledge derived from the artist's sense of what 'fits.' Similarly, David Bohm's lifelong effort to reconstruct science on the basis of wholeness and unity expresses itself most clearly when he employs aesthetic metaphors to describe how 'fitness' implies unity and wholeness.[17] John Dewey's scientific instrumentalism eventually yields to his insight that art is a better vector for carrying his message of the importance of consummatory experience for the creation of lasting human values.[18] Whitehead calls his whole metaphysical project a "critique of pure feeling,"[19] and Merleau-Ponty eventually turns to art to deepen his sense of the importance of feeling in human development.[20]

But it is not enough to provide a list of philosophers. What does happen when images express our experience of the real? When images express themselves, they do so by restructuring experience into a foreground/background gestalt. This provides the necessary individuality for the inscape of Soul to find expression. Vivid unique expression is the hallmark of Soul. But it is precisely here at this moment of self-expression that the danger of lost connections emerges. It is critical that the image retains concrete contact with the background. When this vital contrast is lost, individuality has erased community, and what is left is mere eccentricity. Or worse, a narcissistic Soul arises, and its various expressions kill all possibility of human growth and development. The integration of Soul's experiences is brought about by feelings rather than any purely physical causes. It is this affective dimension that makes the factor of the integer both possible and powerful. By binding together the varieties of feelings felt by Soul, the integer makes a one out of many. The integer takes many forms ranging from the divine grace cited by Augustine in his *Confessions* to the chance meeting of James Joyce and Nora Barnacle on a Dublin street. Whenever it occurs, we find the unfolding expression of a human Soul seeking to change both its own character and its environment. The process is long, difficult, and calls for the utmost in human strength.

In his journals Hopkins echoes Plato and Whitehead; he speaks of "selving," instress, "pitch," and finally "play and field." Each expression deepens the meaning of inscape and thereby the concept of Soul now emerging. These are 'feeling' expressions and immediately convey the effort and drama involved in Soul's work. Hopkins stresses the fact that Soul is always in the process of becoming and not an already achieved substance. "Selving" expresses the ongoing creation of what I have termed the "Soul-self." Its qualities are not accidental to its being. The forms used to integrate the various occasions of its experience cause an "instress" in its inscape such that the lines and integuments developed during its selving are the very signature of its coming to be. Straining to do justice to its values, the Soul-self leaves expressive tracks. These marks depict its triumphs and failures. The fame of the philosopher Duns Scotus rests on his power to unravel these expressions of a Soul's efforts.[21] In so instressing our Souls, we achieve a pitch of being not unlike Spinoza's *conatus*. But it is not all strain and effort, for the achievement of self is also likened to playing in a field. There is a tune carried by Soul, and to hear it one must be able to play in a field. Recall the musical "hoot" whispered by the slave. The field is our personal environment and worldly conditions. This field is alive with feelings. Every image, perception, and idea carries along with it a feeling tone. Emotions clothe our conscious modes of becoming. This is why this chapter began with Hopkins' words.

The looked for bonds between brain and mind, Soul and body reside in these feelings. This is the reason the choice of expressions is so important. The key to the discovery of feelings rests in our ability to put them into expressive forms. The poet and all other artists do this as part of their genius. They play in the fields of expression and thereby give birth to Soul in its myriad forms. Plato's forms are not caskets for the dead. Nor are they abstractions dwelling in another timeless realm. As earlier said, forms breathe fire into the universe. When images are vested in feelings, they are the converse of dried up dead things. As Whitehead says they are like the dry bones in the Old Testament's book of Ezekiel: "So I prophesied as he commanded me, and the breath came into them, and they lived, and stood up upon their feet, an exceeding great army."[22] Philosophy is the attempt at the sheer disclosure of Soul as it expresses its form throughout the universe.

In previous writings I have spoken of the need to cultivate an art of felt intelligence so that the feeling base of experience can be lifted out of its hiding places. This 'invisible world' is the heart of value expressing intense feelings that announce the arrival of new forms of creativity. *Nature, The City,* and now *Soul* as 'Expression' are efforts to bring to public attention this place where Soul lives. The "hard problem" of consciousness and the "explanatory gap" that so bedevils many materialistic philosophers of mind will neither be solved nor sealed until the expression of feelings finds a place in the methodology of science. As I have argued elsewhere, the East is far ahead of Western science when it comes to creating ways to develop this art of felt intelligence.[23] The cultivation of inner feelings through meditation is a treasure trove that science is just beginning to explore.[24]

But an important obstacle remains. Consider the characteristics of Soul as dealt with earlier: subjectivity, intensity of feeling, creativity, integration and transformation, and personal unity. One cannot find within these dimensions of Soul any mention of 'the other.' So far a solitary portrait of Soul has been painted. Its expressions have been confined to its own self-assertions. And its goal has been to separate itself from others through a fierce expression of individuality. *Haecceitas* is a sign of strength but it also can hang itself out to dry. Soul's inscape is not exhausted by the solitary expression of one's own way of life. Such atomic individualism is contrary to any really human way of being. As Aristotle told us, that person who lives alone may very well be a god or may also be a beast, but it is a certainty that such a person is no human being. For humans are meant to dwell together.[25]

Eventually Soul will be understood to be a unique form of harmony that weaves its being out of the conditions and circumstances of its situations. This act of composition takes up the reality of others and merges it into its own way of being. Soul's agony and Soul's joy take rise from the need to recognize others and be recognized by the same. It lives out the passion of the slave and the despair of the master that Hegel argued was the beginning of Soul making.[26] Freedom and autonomy depend upon proper acknowledgment of each other. Self-consciousness arises when the other recognizes the value of its opposing human being. Dialectical experience is the radical form of harmony that Soul uses to grow into its own genius and self-worth. All this is a fancy philosophical way of saying what we already know: *we need each other*. God found Paradise unsuited for his solitary creation. It is not good for man to be alone. The health of Soul depends upon its concord with others. It draws strength from its experiences with difference. A life of sameness is boring and stifling. Sapped of dynamic force Soul lacks the power it needs to become itself. Its singularity suffers in the absence of others. This tells us much about the difficulty of drawing just the right portrait of the workings of Soul. A universal definition may only offer a hollow sameness and along with it, an emptiness that fails to mirror back the unique inscape that is the mark of each and every Soul. Without a rich source of difference to draw upon, the 'thisness' so necessary for genuine Soul making is inaccessible. Unique self-creation is impossible. A literally 'Soulless' person becomes the standard issue of the human race. And what comes to the fore as the archetype of the person of genuine quality is the commonplace, the usual, the run of the mill, the mundane, the regular, the expected, the typical, the undistinguished, the unremarkable, the routine, the conventional, the traditional, the conformist, the predictable, the banal, the boring, the monotonous, the humdrum, the wearisome, the tiresome, the mind-numbing, the dreary, the dull, the tedious, the insipid, the trite, the undead, the zombie, the man in the gray flannel suit, the professional—in short, the square.

I believe that it was a feeling of agonizing loneliness or mind-numbing boredom that drove John of the Cross out into the streets on that legendary "Dark Night." Here I repeat again in a special translation by a Mexican Sister working with the poor in the South Bronx of New York City the first stanza of "The Dark Night of the Soul":

> On a dark night,
> Filled with anxiety
> On fire with love
> By luck, I got away unnoticed
> My house still well guarded.

—John of the Cross [Translation by Sister Juanita, Hermanas de San Jeronimo, Iglesia de San Jeronimo, South Bronx, New York]

2

INVOLVEMENT

> Soul . . . has its source in the First and thence, along an unhindered path, it flows into a total of things, conferring grace, and, because it remains one same thing occupied in one task, dominating.
>
> —Plotinus, *Ennead* IV.4. 10

"Thereby modern philosophy has been ruined."[1] This sounds like Nietzsche on a good day (or maybe a bad one). Prepare for an electric shock: it was Alfred North Whitehead, grand conciliator and irenic system builder, who spoke those damning words. And what is more, he spoke them during his inaugural Lowell Lectures at Harvard University in 1925. What could have driven such a careful thinker to make so daring and yet so self-assured a pronouncement? I believe the answer lies in the fact that Whitehead, as we Americans like to say, had "had it" with the philosophy practiced on both sides of the Atlantic by his predecessors and his contemporaries. As we know Whitehead took the idea of philosophy as a speculative adventure very seriously. He could no longer deal with a worldview that had grown sterile and effete. The rest of the quotation tells us what he was reacting against: "It [philosophy] has oscillated in a complex manner between three extremes. There are the dualists, who accept matter and mind on an equal basis, and the two varieties of monists, those who put mind inside matter and those who put matter inside mind. But this juggling with abstractions can never overcome the inherent confusion introduced by the ascription of *misplaced concreteness* to the scientific scheme of the seventeenth century."[2] My earlier studies, *Nature* and the *City*, relied on the category

of pattern to build up the world of concrete experience. So far this study has been content to describe Soul as solitary and uniquely itself. But among the characteristics of Soul listed in the last chapter were two features—integration and transformation. Both activities are critical for understanding how Soul establishes patterns and makes contact with the world. In order to enrich the contacts of Soul with the actual world, it is necessary to introduce a new category in this discussion. The patterns of Soul are to be understood as modes of involvement. Soul's double character as integration and transformation expresses itself as involvement. But even as I write these words that are meant to alter our understanding of Soul, the habits of the modern mind assert themselves with a stubborn force. I am tempted to write "body and Soul" or "body and mind." Once these abstractions invade our consciousness, all the old dualisms come charging along to keep them company. It seems to be all but impossible to keep from committing and recommitting the fallacy of misplaced concreteness. As Whitehead in the very same Lowell Lecture describes the situation:

> It has held its own as the guiding principle of scientific studies ever since. It is still reigning. Every university organizes itself in accordance with it. No alternative system of organizing the pursuit of scientific truth has been suggested. It is not only reigning, but it is without a rival.
>
> And yet—it is quite unbelievable. This conception of the universe is surely framed in terms of high abstractions, and the paradox only arises because we have mistaken our abstractions for concrete realities.[3]

In the face of these implacable forces, how are we to name these "concrete realities"? Go back to the slave field. What is there most concretely is *the experience of the expression of feeling*. Soul's involvement with the world is bathed in the experience of the expression of feeling. I propose that we examine Soul's involvement with reality in four different ways. These ways are drawn from Whitehead's theory of orders as laid out in *Process and Reality*. Such a description has the decided advantage of using the experience of the expression of feeling as the primary medium for grasping concrete reality. These four orders are derived from human feelings and tie together involvement, patterns, and orders as modes of experience. I intend to propose an alternative to the fallacy of misplaced concreteness.

Soul's involvement in the world of concrete realities takes shape within four dominant orders of experience: the trivial, the vague, the narrow, and the wide. Each order has its own levels, and each also has the capacity to combine with the others. All orders are to some degree present in every concrete reality. The orders to be discussed are basic ones that can be directly experienced as such, but they also are "logically vague" in the sense that their full understanding requires a reference to specific situations and conditions. I can say there will be dinner, but I can also say there will be baked haddock for dinner. The former is logically vague; the latter adds specificity and thereby provides a fuller understanding of what is happening. In the slave field we can have a vague idea of the punishing cruelty of slave labor. But to feel directly and intensely what is "going on," we need to know what that 'hoot' is all about.

Patterns of order dominate Soul's relation to the concrete world of human feelings.[4] In turn Soul's reaction to these orders elicits kinds and levels of feeling. Thus trivial orders render experience indifferent. Vague orders induce moods of expectation that something is about to happen. Narrow orders summon up intense feelings from Soul. And finally, wide orders demand Soul's significant involvement. What is it about these orders that makes them function in such distinctive ways? Each pattern of order lays out a specific way in which existential reality grips Soul. Trivial orders suggest nothing special about their members. In fact within the pattern of the trivial nothing grabs Soul's attention. One could say that in the region of the trivial nothing is important, or what is the same thing, everything is important. When everything is judged important, the uniqueness of importance is lost.

Vague orders shift the feelings of Soul in the direction of the emergence of something important. Selective dimensions of the situation begin to stand out and a form of 'profundity' gains attention. Still this form of order is a mild one in the sense that the unity expressed is of the loosest kind. Here there is an invitation to imagine possibilities and to sense alternative modes of being. Vagueness is the first step toward organization for it allows Soul to feel the real presence of a potential harmony. The feeling of expectation is a necessary prologue to the growth and development of the human Soul.

Narrow orders make demands on Soul. They point in a single direction and promise intensity of experience and in effect toss alternatives to the side. They are, as it were, 'all-or-nothing' propositions. One stands to lose great intensity if the narrow path is shunned. Narrowness is in agreement with those dimensions of Soul's inscape that express uniqueness and rich, powerful individuality. In terms of achieving direct forceful expression, narrow patterns are among the Soul's optimum avenues of experience. Still: exclusion is the price to be paid for richness of direct experience. No doubt the junkie has an impressively intense experience, but the elimination of alternatives is a very high price to pay for such rewards. Also it is not to be forgotten that narrowness ultimately costs Soul its range of experienced feelings of expression. The constraints placed on Soul's creativity by patterns of narrowness suggest that there should be better configurations of experience.

Width is the remaining order that Soul may have the opportunity to experience. Here one must be careful. Width is not to be confused with shallow. It is the very opposite of superficial experience. To confuse width with one-dimensional experience is to convert it into the trivial. And that turns Soul back to the beginnings of its search for the experience of the expression of feelings. There has been no gain in the texture of Soul's experience. Width comes about when narrowness is woven onto vagueness. The weaving necessary to express width summons up new creative forces of expression, and in this sense width is the equivalent of depth. At this point the aptness of drawing on involvement as the touchstone of Soul's experience becomes evident. Successful experience in the domain of width ties together the experiential threads bound up in the situation at hand. It expresses importance without narrowing it down to a single element. It expresses intensity without blotting out alternative pathways. Most importantly it allows for a fresh way of understanding involvement.

That fresh way is the concept of harmony that will become prominent as this study progresses. Harmony does not mean something pretty, nice, or sweet. It is both an idea and an image, and it unites both thinking and feeling. A harmony is a unique way of bringing together events that are usually considered incompatible. Examples are different colors, musical notes, ideas, and types of legal authority, social classes, personal feelings, and so on. The list could be indefinitely extended. All harmonies have in common the fact that they bring into unity what was previously separated. A harmony is a response to the problem of the one and the many. The degree of its success depends upon the degree of simplicity and complexity the harmonic resolution is able to sustain. The normative measure for judging harmonies is "The greater the union of the one and the many without losing the uniqueness of either the complex or the simple, the greater the intensity of feeling achieved by the event in question." Involvement is therefore best carried out through the creation of harmonic events.

Our theme is integration and transformation for they are the actions that move Soul out of itself. Both forms of action can be carried out poorly or well. Any satisfactory action demands the capacity to measure well, but it is of essential importance when it comes to acts of harmony. Without a correct sense of what is being dealt with, acts of integration and transformation are doomed from the outset. At this point intelligence enters the picture. But what kind of intelligence is needed to measure well Soul's involvement with the world? I suggest that it has everything to do with gaining a "feel" for what is going on. Chinese philosophers speak of the "propensities of things," and that is very close to what I am suggesting as a necessary element of Soul power.

I have elsewhere named this capacity to take the measure of situations *felt intelligence*.[5] This means that measurement requires evaluation. The key to adequate evaluation lies in the ability to feel the expression of value put forth by the event in question. The measure of this value resides in the intensity of the feeling created by Soul's integrative and transformative powers. In *Adventures of Ideas* Whitehead discusses two types of harmony, both of which are enlisted to express what is distinctive about forms of beauty. The first type is relatively meek for it involves tamping down differences for the sake of creating a tame harmony. Direct clashes of value are avoided, but the price paid is enough to bankrupt civilization's pursuit of value. Whitehead calls the result of this type of expression of feeling, "anesthesia."[6] In other words expression has disappeared and with it any genuine trace of Soul.

But there is also what Whitehead calls "the major form of beauty." Here we encounter the experience of Soul in its most powerful expression. What distinguishes this harmony from all others is its creative force. As I said in the previous chapter, it reaches below the depths of things and brings forth a novel intensity of expression. So novel, in fact, that ordinary words fail, and what is required is a new mode of expression—one not yet experienced on this planet.

> Think back to Rilke's "Archaic Torso of Apollo." And its demand for transformation: "You must change your life."
>
> Sense the wild call of daylight's invitation to follow it in Dylan's "jingle jangle morning . . ."
>
> Feel the stupefying scream of the wounded horse in Picasso's "Guernica."

The hypothesis is that Soul is expression and that efforts to do away with it in favor of other concepts such as body (brain) or mind are doomed to keep philosophy penned up in its own stable of abstractions. What is more, Soul can also be envisioned as an act of primordial harmony—one that engages the world through integration and transformation. Involvement is of the essence of Soul. In addition to being well formed, a hypothesis must be tested. What kind of truth can be expected from this hypothesis that the Soul is expression and that harmony is the means by which its expressive powers are maximized? Whitehead has a response: "The type of Truth required for the final stretch of beauty is a discovery and not a recapitulation. The Truth that for such an extremity of beauty is wanted is that truth-relation whereby Appearance summons up new resources for feeling from the depths of reality. It is a truth of feeling, and not a truth of verbalization. The relata in Reality must lie below the stale presuppositions of verbal thought. The Truth of supreme beauty lies beyond the dictionary meaning of words."[7] These words widen expression beyond words, widen it beyond signs and symbols, widen it beyond the acts of nature and, finally, so widen it as to make expression the very meaning of process as reality.

But if harmony is the meaning of involvement understood as transformation and integration, what is the source of its strength? What lets harmony be so powerful that it can both integrate and transform situations? Harmony is often thought of, wrongly, as the absence of conflict. It is not merely sweetness in song or music. Harmony, as discussed above, is the royal road to intensity. It is strength, power, authority, command, rule, energy, and force. From what patterns of involvement do such qualities arise? There is a great paradox here for what gives harmony its force is individuality.

I began this chapter with Whitehead's condemnation of abstractions masquerading as concrete universals. There is a similar fallacy at play here in the question of individuality and harmony. Remember Hume linked his empiricism to not just bare sensations but also to their expression in terms of universals. This effectively bars the way for any philosophical discussion of particulars. Whether the dress is red or old or of this particular design is of no consequence because when it came to discussion of the dress, only universals could be used. In effect *this* dress was thrown out of court. As a matter of fact any reference to *this* particular dress was invalid. The universal in its bare abstractness swallowed up the particular. The irony here is that a fact (which is empiricism's touchstone) is kept from ever appearing in the philosophical discourse sanctioned by the doctrines of empiricism. Facts are singular, particular, bound to this space and this time. Universals are the opposite for they sweep up rough-edged facts and embalm them in airtight containers.

It is here that Whitehead's doctrine of the power of the "*IT*" comes into significant play. It will be recalled that vague orders of being demand further specification if their full truth and value are to be expressed. This concern for the particular reinforces *inscape* as the meaning of Soul. The following quotation sums up with precise concreteness the contributions donated by the "*ITS*" of this world:

> [O]ur lives are dominated by the enduring things, each experienced as a unity of many occasions bound together by the force of inheritance. Each such individual endurance collects into its unity the shifting qualities of its many occasions. Perhaps it is the thing we love, or perhaps it is the thing we hate. There is a bare *It*—a real fact of the past, stretching into the present, which concentrates upon itself the wealth of emotion derived from its many occasions. Such enduring individualities, as factors in experience, control a wealth of feeling, amplitude of purpose, and a regulative power to subdue into the background the residue of things belonging to the immensity of the past.[8]

To identify and experience such "*ITS*" is one function of the felt intelligence discussed in *Nature* and *The City*. Each situation, environment, ecological niche, and even person has its peculiar feel. A Soul in full possession of its powers is able to experience the expression of that feeling. When this occurs, genuine, authentic involvement has taken place. When true to its black roots, American culture has immediately recognized and understood the connection between vivid experience and Soul. It is this sensibility that is at the heart of the doctrine of harmony. It is detail that carries feelings through environments that would otherwise reduce or even eliminate their intensity.

Soul murder is committed when the strength provided by vivid detail is lost or forgotten or pushed aside by other cultural pressures. Once again, it is a case of narrowness weaving its way through vagueness so as to create width and depth of experience. Soul involves itself in the world when it is freed to concentrate on particular aspects of human experience. When it does so successfully, rich and powerful character arises. The identity Soul fashions for itself is largely due to its capacity to honor and enhance the inscapes of the world. In so doing it intensifies its own being, and vibrant expressions of value take root in personal, social, and cultural life.

Soul is the art of composition. Artists know beauty is the fortunate combination of width and depth. Width is provided by openings to possibility, and depth is secured when possibility finds actual expression in factually concrete features. But intensity of feeling is no guarantee of truth, and truth is needed for strong enduring value. Living a lie is just another form of Soul murder. It is individual facts that make fast the truth relation. As a factual 'this' rather than a false 'that,' the "*IT*" character of harmony assures authentic expression in a real world. Empty universals remain just that—void of actuality, sheer potentials that await realization through Soul's efforts. There is no sadder proof for the truth of this way of understanding harmony than the present tragedy of Iraq. We are at war, but few civilians act as if we were. Shopping, games, and plans go on as if there were no lives lost or maimed. The reason for this fiasco is the fact that the public at large experiences few if any details of this horror show. To quote Whitehead: "At the base of experience there is a welter of feeling, derived from individual realities or directed towards them."[9] When citizens are prevented from experiencing the actual results of government policies, civilization becomes a potential killing ground awaiting those clever enough to fill it with their illusions.

It is precisely here that truth expresses its importance. The 'truth' born forward by universals is really only generalizations. Generals tend to generalize. They thwart emotional response by reason of their residence in the realm of the possible. Affect is lost, and feeling is diminished as an empty deadness slides over society. We are talking here about massive cultural amnesia induced by the dominance of abstractions taken to be concrete realities. That which is neither true nor false overwhelms Soul. How can authentic involvement take place when the real loses all touch with the actual? Dreams arise and are proclaimed. They remain dreams or, in the case of Iraq, nightmares. Conviction is confined to universal ideas that gain no purchase in reality. Even imagination loses its power for the mind's eye has nothing to see or envision. There are no connections to be made between this discrete object and the next item brought to our attention. The magic of modern advertising relies upon this division between the particular and the universal. It supplies bogus connections, and imaginations are stirred by the link between an auto and sex, beer and joy, buildings and universities. The image replaces the real because the possible is disguised by the actual. This is the reason Plato opposed the sophists. They offered false goods and then had the 'chutzpah' to charge for it. Today many of us buy into this masquerade.

Understanding Soul is the aim of this book. By now it should be evident that Soul is in danger. What to do? The truth is the answer. But remember that convinced skeptic Pilate who did indeed wash his hands. Truth has many dimensions and flourishes in many places, but Soul truth has to do with value. When bare universals (like body and mind) are substituted for individual facts, process as the expression of vibrant feeling can no longer be felt. To use two of the dominant universals of our time, we become brain dead and mindless. To use a much more integrated phrase: *The ability to feel is lost.* Human beings take on the character of zombies, beings without Souls. Just as too much feeling drowns the Soul in overheated waters of intensity, so also too little makes a desert of what should be a river of life. How then does truth serve harmony so as to balance Soul's involvement in the world?

Truth is the way in which value is carried over from the past into the present and into the relevant future. Value has already been defined as intensity of experience. The importance of truth for Soul's involvement is evident. Truth gives enduring strength and direction to the harmony created by Soul. It does this by pointing out what is an appropriate involvement for the situation at hand.[10] Any human situation has three temporal dimensions: the past that harbors its origins, the present that is the scene of its creative actions, and the future that it seeks to influence. Soul's judgment as to how it will construct its involvement demands the unification of knowledge and action. To know is not confined to understanding. Knowledge arises within and expresses itself through action. The unity of knowledge and action is a well-known aspect of American pragmatism and is expressed most clearly in the thought of John Dewey. What is less well known is its ancient and distinguished history. It is powerfully expressed in the work of the NeoConfucian philosopher Wang Yang-ming. Wang's battle cry was: "*holi wan fu jujin,*" the unity of knowledge and action.

The symmetry that exists between Wang, Dewey, and this exploration of Soul is located in a shared metaphysical vision. Philosophy's history has always harbored schools of philosophy that reject Aristotle's proposal that contemplative serenity ought to be the goal of the philosopher's life. The insistence to emphasize facts and to find the forms in the facts runs counter to Aristotle's claim that the philosopher's vocation is confined to the discovery and articulation of universal ideas. Philosophers who insist that action is an essential ingredient in the acquisition and recognition of truth are committed to a vision of process as the meaning of reality. When becoming replaces being as the touchstone of the real, then action becomes a necessary dimension of knowledge. Action is particular and aimed at the specifics of a situation; otherwise, it is just a lot of gas. Here is the reason for Whitehead's rejections of universals as the sole carrier of experience. The concrete is the actual; the universal is the possible. Both are required for an adequate metaphysics. Everything depends on establishing the right relation between these two dimensions of the real. Half a millennium beforehand, Wang Yang-ming said it more dramatically: "*chih hsing hoi*," knowledge and action are really one.[11] There is no intellectual state prior to knowing and there is no bodily state prior to doing. Both are abstractions made actual within the integrating efforts of the human person. Sincerity and integrity harmonize within the HeartMind of the acting person. Experience does not begin with sensation, nor is it initiated by reasoning. Concrete knowledge is the gift of our interactions with situations. We learn to teach by teaching. We learn to hit a baseball by hitting it. We learn a poem by reading it aloud. And so on and so on.

The appropriate relation must be carried out by action and not by possibilities. We are here talking about the essence of experience. It is John Dewey who identified the basic elements of experience. He said that experience was double-barreled. It is both a doing and an undergoing. Soul acts by transforming situations into harmonies, and in so doing it encounters resistance, refusal, and rejection. It undergoes suffering. Through the effort required to bring resolution to a situation, the direct meaning of the unity of knowledge and action is concrete experiences. How, Wang would say (and Dewey would second him), could we know anything unless we interact with it?[12]

No unification of knowledge can be carried out without the active participation of authentic individuals. This brings the discussion back to the importance of the *IT*. Once again detail expressing its own uniqueness moves value through the intricacies of existence. Inscape is the essential factor in great experiences. It is not a home run. It is Willie Mays who hit the home run, and it is we who carry Willie along in his experience of rounding the bases. There is a genuine unification of the ball player and our selves. Thinking is experiencing, and acting is experiencing. Soul is the expression of the feeling of this miraculous unity. The act of living demands participation in what we are not; therefore, knowledge, be it habitual or reflective, is necessary to survive. To thrive demands a higher unification of knowledge and action. This is the point at which harmony asserts its signature importance in the growth of Soul. It is the refined adjustments and the recurrent need for changing attunements that establish harmony as Soul's most creative expression. A process world is always "on the go," and its harmonies must be resourceful, novel, and enduring. Lumbering social institutions have a most difficult time catching up. It is the imaginative individual that is most often in demand. In establishing the artist as the prototype of the valuable citizen, Dewey tacitly acknowledges Soul's work as the art of composition.

Chinese sensibility has long been attuned to the importance of the aesthetic feel of worldly situations. The great Western Inscription of Chang Tsai reads: "Heaven is my father and Earth is my mother and even such a small creature as I find an intimate place in their midst."[13] Knowing the reverence that the Chinese hold for their ancestors, it is apparent how important it is to treat one's situations with respect and care. The same emotional tone affects Wang Yang-ming's insistence on the unity of knowledge and action. Harmony is respect for the elements that are to be combined so as to bring about a higher good. Process thought is a metaphysics of experience for it makes experience the standard for understanding the myriad interactions that make up the world. Experience, done well, heals gaps and unifies what has been separated. It directly challenges human beings. It demands that the edges of egotism be softened for the sake of including what is different into what is happening. Experience toughens the idea of harmony for, as Dewey never failed to point out, all genuine experience adds up to a transformation that involves both doing and undergoing. The doing is clear enough, for the individual must take hold of what is and refashion it so as to mesh the old with the new. Undergoing is a different matter, for we are not accustomed to mark out the suffering that is so very much a part of experience. To transform is also to be transformed. And recalling the Western Inscription, we are dealing with our mother and father and not some neutral piece of matter. Bringing together knowledge and action requires a deft hand. It is never a matter of forcing a situation.

Soul works to create harmonies where vicious separations exist. The features of Soul discussed in chapter 1 are subjectivity, intensity of feeling, creativity, integration, transformation, and personal unity. Each feature derived its creative power from Soul's primary process as the expression of feeling. Each of these features, in its own way, contributes to the unity of action and knowledge that brings about harmonies of experience. Without their active presence Soul would be powerless to involve itself in worldly experience. Subjectivity makes possible the need for individuality in the acts of involvement generated by Soul. Centers of organization resist the drift inherent in a process universe. Order and the coordination of orders that lend weight and endurance to the universe's ever shifting intensities of value are a needed counterbalance to the transience endemic in the process of becoming. Subjectivity geared to the preservation of value is needed if truth as the carryover of value is to emerge. Similarly, authentic intensity of feeling depends upon its place of safety in the truth. This follows directly from the next feature of Soul, creativity. In aiming at the full expression of feelings Soul can fall into tragic illusions. Truth can catch Soul before such misdirection can occur. Integration and transformation are the ways with which Soul creates the harmonies needed for intense living. Finally, personal unity, a gift of the factor of the integer, renders the processes of harmonic creativity whole. These ways of Soul making rest upon the unity of knowledge and action that has been under discussion. In the previous chapter I introduced Susanne Langer's concept of the 'act' as the primordial moment of Soul life. Along with the act came the need for the creation of images to convey the feelings that are at the heart of mind. Putting these ideas together renders the unity of knowledge and action more concretely understandable. Images evoke feelings. Feelings are the ground of mind, but they also can poison Soul through enchantment and infatuation. Action and its results are the antidote. But feeling, knowing, and acting are the sum and substance of Soul at work. It follows that Soul's personal unity is necessary if it is to be true to its expressive vocation.

Character develops through continual efforts at achieving personal unity. Moral excellence cannot be dismissed as mere refinement. It is not to be ignored by the person or the social order. It is what makes a wholehearted life possible. At the same time it secures an opening for the potential emergence of the felt presence of goodness, beauty, and truth. The individual details (the "*ITS*") that made involvement real are also the material of human behavior. *Ethos*, as the Greeks called it, is the fruit of the unity of knowledge and action. Just as Soul is the source of individual creativity, so also can it become a moral force when human involvement is at work. I believe this is why Spinoza expressed his metaphysics as *Ethics* and why Heidegger failed to provide an answer to the question of the meaning of being.

This chapter on involvement began with an analysis of Whitehead's rejection of empty abstractions as the way to carry out philosophical reflection. In place of such empty universals he offered a program that looked for individual details as the key to the effective creation of harmonies. Using these suggestions I have attempted to open up an alternative inquiry concerning the human Soul. There is a paradox at work in this examination of involvement. It was begun because the first chapter left Soul isolated in its inscape. To remedy that situation this chapter has concentrated on the act of involvement. But this chapter began with Whitehead's dissatisfaction with philosophy's reliance on empty universals to tie the world of events together. Such a method led directly to the fallacy of misplaced concreteness that has paralyzed discussion of the integration of the human person. To correct this flaw individuality in its richness of expression has been introduced. Does this not return us to the loneliness we left at the end of chapter 1?

The proper response to this question harks back to the idea of harmony as requiring strong and enduring individuality so as to promote maximum intensity of feeling. The principle of individuality conjoined to the doctrine of harmony does away with the threat of alienated existence. Harmony invested with the strength of real individuals is the process whereby concrete involvement can enter the world. The unity of knowledge and action as well as feeling and value are vividly expressed in these words of Whitehead:

> Thus, the basis of a strong penetrating experience of Harmony is an Appearance with a foreground of enduring individuals carrying with them a force of subjective tone, and with a background of providing the requisite connection. Undoubtedly, the Harmony is finally a Harmony of qualitative feelings. But the introduction of the enduring individuals evokes from the Reality a force of already harmonized feelings which no surface show of sensa can produce. It is not a question of intellectual interpretation. There is a real conflation of fundamental feeling.[14]

The concept of 'appearance' is dealt with in the next chapter. Here at the end of this discussion of Soul's involvement it is important to underscore the vital importance of intense feeling for a true understanding of Soul's participation in the world. Without feeling Soul is not really there.

Every time we are affected by a work of art intense feelings are experienced. Read Rilke's heart stopping poem, *The Panther*. One cannot but be sent reeling by its conclusion: ". . . plunges into the heart and is gone." And here is Rilke revealing to his wife the source of his involvement in the life of this captured animal:

> In his studio in the rue de l'Universite, Rodin has a tiny plaster cast of a tiger (antique) that he values very highly. . . . There is in this animal the same kind of aliveness as in the modeling [what Rilke witnessed in Rodin's studio]; on this little Thing (it is no higher than my hand is wide, and no longer than my hand is) there are a hundred thousand places, as if it were really huge—a hundred thousand places that are all alive, active, and different. All this just in plaster! And

the representation of the prowling stride is intensified to the highest degree, the powerful downward tread of the broad paws, and simultaneously that caution in which all strength is wrapped, that noiselessness.[15]

And so we move toward the capability that made this expression possible, consciousness.

3

FEELING THE ALTERNATIVES

What gives Soul its bounce? The answer is human consciousness. The great gift bestowed on Soul by consciousness is *the sense of the alternative*. The feeling that something else can be or might be is the result of feeling the contrasts that are at work in the world of process. Consciousness fuses two opposites, the actual facts and the possible alternatives, and thereby creates a third way of being.

I am driving home and am not conscious of all that I am doing. The road is so familiar and the operation of the car so habitual that I am, as is said, on automatic pilot. Suddenly, a huge truck swerves into my path. What comes to mind so quickly that it is scarcely measurable is a sense of the alternative. What presents itself to me is a *what is* joined to a *what can be* and a *what might be*. I am now conscious.

Admittedly the example is dramatic, but it contains all the elements needed to grasp the phenomenon of consciousness. First, there is the indifference that is my state of feeling as I drive home. Then there is the sudden emergence of difference that counters my previous sensibility. Finally, there is recognition that an alternative has emerged out of the comfortable jumble of feelings that have accompanied me on the way home. Whitehead's definition of this unique experience is "the affirmation of a negation."[1] This compressed phrase is laden with meaning. It holds the key to Soul's growth as well as an alternative way of understanding the mind-body problem that so bedevils contemporary philosophy. What has occurred in my drive is experience. It is this that must be kept in mind as we explore the relation between Soul and consciousness. Human awareness arises when an integrated contrast between a fact (my driving and the truck's appearance) and a theory (a fast turn to the left may help me avoid a collision) is directly felt. Before that experience my awareness was immersed in routine activities. Consciousness emerged when stubborn fact invaded my world and demanded a response from me. Depending on the quality of my awareness a number of responses could have occurred. I might have continued ahead and died. I might have avoided the truck and lived. The point is integration between stubborn fact, "I" and "might" and "action" took place.

The integration was between an actuality and a possibility. They fused at that moment, and awareness jumped into my experience. I felt a powerful sense of an alternative. It was not my brain that experienced this felt contrast, nor was it my mind. During this moment my "body" is an abstraction, and so is my mind. In the concreteness of this moment neither body nor mind is the sole concrete agent at work. What is concretely felt right here now is a moment of experience. Within the integrated contrast that is this moment Soul expresses itself through the feelings felt and the actions undertaken. It is not the brain that is thinking. It is not mind that is put on view. Soul is right here at that moment expressing itself.

We are one integrated process. We are not solely a mind or solely a body. That is monism. We are not a body *and* a mind. That is dualism. And we are not at that moment a behavioral function. That is a Soulless depiction that leaves out the 'I.' In dealing with the contrasts that are the constituent components of consciousness, we are confronted with a way of being that is not easily expressed by means of a conventional subject-predicate language. There is too much liveliness and action calling for concrete expression. Elements melt together and then just as suddenly fly apart. There is a flow of energy that reaches a level of awareness so intensely acute that words fail. That is why we resort to images, metaphors, and similes. We experience the feel of the occasion, and then it is gone. It is process itself, but that is also not exactly accurate. We are in the moment of conscious process itself. Soul utters itself as consciousness, and in that moment expression is born. We do not *have* consciousness. We *are* consciousness.[2]

But what is expressed? A sense of the alternative. An affirmation of negation. What do these phrases have to do with Soul? Recall "The Dark Night of the Soul." The inscape of Soul revealed its singularity, and this dominant individuality led to a dark night wherein companionship was sought. Soul's desire for the other led to the projects of involvement described in the previous chapter. The sense of the alternative felt in processes of consciousness provides Soul with the room needed to enlarge its harmonies of inclusion. It is by expansion of awareness that Soul encounters opportunities for growth and development. The forceful presence of consciousness makes possible the acts of change that can lead to enduring transformations of Soul.

It is therefore adjustment, adaptation, and change of attitude that are the genuine signatures of transformation. By itself awareness can do little to express the workings of Soul. That mode of expression is the subject of the next chapter. One need only read Hegel's description of the "Beautiful Soul" in the *Phenemenology* to understand the debilitation induced by expanded consciousness annulled by ineffective action. Or to bring the matter closer to home, think what happens when a powerful presence flies into town, tells everyone what to do, and then flies out again. Such preachers, teachers, and politicians have a very cushy job. They tell Souls what to do and then leave!

Such acts of deceit produce a double misfortune. These moral cheerleaders are encouraged to repeat their performances in the next town or city. But at the same time their hearers become filled with a profound self-loathing as their efforts to take up these empty challenges fail for lack of support. The root of this problem is falsehood, deception, and lies. What is at stake in generating a feel for the alternative is the truth relation. Human awareness provides various types of appearance, so the relation between reality and appearance becomes critical. Falsehood weakens Soul's presence in the real. It corrodes Soul's power to transform itself. It seduces Soul onto paths that lead to destruction or worse. It smiles on folly and encourages Soul to do the same. It makes a game out of the serious business of living a life. It offers delusion and illusion and names these imposters as real. In our culture it has been given a new name: spin.

There are many types of truth, but the type of truth that concerns us here is that involved in the creation of harmony.[3] Recall that harmony is the way in which openness is created so that more and more richness of experience can be poured into Soul's experience without losing balance and equilibrium. Understood this way, it reinforces Whitehead's use of Plato's concept of the 'receptacle' as expressed in the *Timaeus*. Harmony needs space if it is to do justice to the variety of emergent values in a process universe. Harmony also involves the use of imagination, which is not necessarily concerned with what is truthful and in fact can be the seed of illusion. The strength of harmony as an instrument for good or evil can be seen in the fact that a harmony is already a contrast. Now if consciousness is a felt contrast, then a harmony is a double contrast. Furthermore as we have already seen, great harmonies are braced by the strong presence of individualities. In our times such "attention getters" are the breath of life for a consumer culture. Always and everywhere we are shown individual things that promise to light up our lives and bring us further down the road of happiness. But it is true that consciousness must be provoked into being. It stands at the end of a long process of experience and need not emerge with any force. The felt sense of an alternative sails between Scylla and Charybdis. On one side sing the sirens of consumer capitalism and on the other lurks the complacent life of the anaesthetized.[4] Much danger and many intense feelings of value are involved in the seemingly innocent word *harmony*.

The structure of imagination involves a contrast established between a background and a foreground. The goal of imaginative creations is not truth but engagement and excitement. Also images come in discrete forms. One never finds two images residing at the same time in a healthy consciousness. The structure of imagination deepens its qualitative subjectivity. Only the holder of the image can experience it in its originality. Insofar as an image is a good one, it spills over with feeling. Its primary mission is to gain attention, and when it does so, Soul is enthralled. But is it engaged by the right experience?

Truth has many meanings. There is the truth of propositions and the truth of sense perception. There is also symbolic truth that captures what cannot be expressed in the mere conformation of a sense perception with an observed fact. We are discussing the importance of harmony for the development and growth of Soul. The experience of beauty is another term for the experience of harmony. In *Adventures of Ideas* Whitehead devotes three entire chapters to "Truth," "Beauty," and "Truth and Beauty."[5] The topic is complex, many-sided, and filled with nuances. Nevertheless, for our purposes the following remarks are central and to the point. "the truth-relation remains the simple, direct mode of realizing Harmony. Other ways are indirect, and indirectness is at the mercy of the environment. There is a blunt force about Truth, which . . . is akin to cleanliness—namely, the removal of dirt, which is unwanted irrelevance. The sense of directness which it carries with it, sustains the upstanding individualities so necessary for the beauty of a complex. Falsehood is corrosive."[6] These are powerful words that reach down into the very inscape of Soul. Soul is individuality itself. This singularity needs truth for its continuing development. Lies, deception, and deceit consume the uniqueness of Soul rendering it the same as any other event in the cosmos. This is what brings about the indifference that allows a social order to kill its members with not so much as a blink of an eye or a genuine tear. The effect of falsehood does not stop with capital punishment. It also causes institutions to treat their members with a kind of absolute indifference. This is the falsehood that generates such words as "resources" for human beings. Soulless dealings with Souls kill off what is most distinctive about human beings—their individual worth.[7]

So the uses of imagination do not merely occupy culture with frivolous entertainments. False dealings eat away at the very substance of the human race. When an entire social group becomes complicit in such deceptions, then its values are at an end and what comes next the slightest survey of history's tragedies can tell us. The power to harmonize one's Soul in a truthful manner is the greatest achievement Soul can express. That is why the great civilizations have always paid homage to those who can balance the complex and the simple, the burdensome and what is trouble-free, and make equilibrium out of all the stopovers in between. To balance is to order, and truth needs expression if beauty is to stand its ground against the contraries that oppose it. A human being cannot live an abstraction, and beauty without truth is just as much an abstraction as truth without beauty. To speak of Soul concretely is to mark out its poise and find ways to express it.

If Soul's first act is imagination, then its original spontaneity in the face of reality is critically important. How does one bring together poise and spontaneity? This is the skill achieved by the Daoist adept and the Zen master. At times it may also be the gifted expression of the most ordinary person. The act of politeness, the thoughtful gesture, the taking of the lower place rather than the higher, moving aside to let another pass, and rising to give one's seat to an elder—all these ordinary actions join poise to spontaneity. In the work of the evolutionary neuroscientist Gerard Edelman, we find the physiological formula that lets us accomplish such gracious feats. Edelman has developed a theory of brain degeneracy that promotes reentrant neuronal activities within the brain. This plasticity of function would be impossible without a brain that quite literally flows with purposeful energy. Spontaneity arises because the human brain is always in the process of continually restructuring itself. A network of neurons no matter how massive could not provide the platform of originality that marks Soul's advance into experience. However, a brain so formed as to constantly break down and rebuild itself is precisely engineered to meet novelty with adaptive skills.

Even though, as I said before, he gives away his materialistic bias with such words as *spooks*, I argue that Edelman's brilliant synthesis of cerebral functioning need not be seen as a retreat into a form of reductive materialism. It is his use of patterns to explain these formidable acts of adaptation that to my mind argues for a deeper understanding of Soul as the creator of uniqueness.[8] Soul is needed to carry out these acts of originality in a form that harmonizes with the varying dimensions of space and time of each person's situation. I am simply arguing that there is a very valid physiological theory that makes possible the expressive life of Soul. Damage this structure, and Soul is incapable of growing new ways to express its poise. To have a fluid underpinning that renders the world responsive to our touch is not to reduce the human being to that foundation. Expression has its external side. How else could it be experienced as expression? But what is expressed is meaning, and that dimension of Soul is not just its material manifestation. There ought not to be any shame in calling the expression of meaning a spiritual act. Rather a certain sense of awe should accompany our understanding of what is involved in Soul's expression. Soul is always in the process of recreating itself within its own physiological habitat. And what is more, these acts of originality can be understood as spontaneous moments of imagination giving rise to an endless line of alternatives for Soul's growth and development.

The full scope of harmony's need for truth should now be evident. False turns, dead ends, and fatal errors lurk around every corner of our evolutionary journey. The imaginary is as much a potential source of destruction as it is of creative construction. This stubborn fact should slow the pace of the philosophical movement that has come to be called "deconstruction." The word itself is such a peculiar conjunction of opposing alternatives. Does it promote the destruction of what has been constructed? Or does it encourage the construction of something finer and more humane? Or does it suggest that we can pull off the impossible and do both at the same time? A feeling for the alternative hides in the first two options, but I can find no room for an alternative in the last option. How could imagination destroy and create at the same time? Are we to destroy the village once more in order to save it once more?

Before these questions bring us to the doorstep of language and its possibilities, it is important to examine in more detail the meaning of poise as it relates to Soul as expression. Consider the situation facing Soul. What is faced is conflict. What is needed is contrast. Furthermore this situation is a regular if not an unremitting dimension of human life. A full human life inevitably encounters conflict. What state of awareness would most help Soul search out and then express an appropriate state of consciousness? I suggest that it is the experience of poise.[9] It involves self-assurance so that Soul is not overwhelmed by the forces it faces. Composure is also a necessary quality when it comes to meeting a crisis. This unique moment of original spontaneity ought to bring about a sense of expansive space and time. The quality that is wanted is often called "deliberate" and for good reason. What poise gives a person is the feel for an alternative judgment that is more open than the situation within which one finds oneself. Space and time are stretched so that hurried judgment is replaced by a sense of calm smooth awareness of possibilities. Time not only expands; it also slows down. Superb athletes speak of such a feeling when they are in the midst of the most beleaguered conditions. A baseball traveling at over ninety miles an hour appears like a big balloon just ready to be hit with maximum force. A quarterback hounded by a set of behemoths about to crush him sees the entire field and all its possibilities arranged before him in such an order that he is able to pick out just the right alternative toward which to hurl the ball. A tennis player facing a serve that tops a hundred miles an hour explains that she hits the ball that is in her head and not the ball traveling toward her.

What is going on here? I believe that the only satisfactory explanation is that a feeling for the alternative has come to dominate a human consciousness. More specific examples also suggest themselves: moments of Zen awareness, a martial arts experience, or a tai ch'i exercise. Each of these accounts (and many others) has merit and deserves its own analysis. They appear to involve an experience of living fully and completely in the present. But no matter what experiential form is employed to achieve these states, a fundamental experience must be present at the beginning and during the situation: a feeling for the alternative that expresses a sense of poise. Poise is purposeful but at this concrete moment also paradoxically spontaneous. Neither planning nor reacting is involved. All is done together and all at once. There emerges a distinctive feeling of trust and self-confidence. Soul gives itself completely. This act of self-bestowal holds nothing back. Soul merges with action, and a genuine kind of knowledge is had. Integration has been achieved, and being, doing, and knowing are one.

Here is a listener's description of experiencing Bob Dylan play music:

> "Joey" [a Dylan song] was a surprise and they didn't stop coming. I dunno [sic] bout [sic] all the new fans around who were finally silenced from telling their whacked out Bob tales to one another by the Master at the pinnicle [sic] of his game but from my perspective, he is shining right now. I've seen Bob play for almost thirty years and to watch him at work now is a huge gift. A diamond as big as a shoe don't even measure up to this man in his full musicality, taken completely by the music in the MOMENT, crafting

pictures outa thin air—disappearing into the song. There is nothing left but the song.[10]

I do not think it possible to improve upon this ad hoc "on-the-web" expression of a Soul poised in its self-expression. But notice certain aspects: "He is shining right now," "taken completely by the music," "in the MOMENT," "crafting pictures outa thin air," "disappearing into the song," and finally, "There is nothing left but the song." All that I have been struggling to say is there: *THE SOUL EXPRESSING ITSELF.* If you prefer, recall the marks of the inscape of Soul: Subjectivity, intensity of feeling, creativity, integration and transformation, personal unity. What is most arresting is the manner in which subjectivity and personal unity contribute to intensity of feeling, creativity, and integration and transformation. It cannot be said that the subject disappears or that personal unity gets in the way of the performance. Somehow or other they melt into the integrity of the performance as it creates a moment of extraordinary intensity of feeling through expressive transformation. These are mere words that can only lamely suggest what happened. We shall revisit this scene, but for now let the experience simply express itself.

Poise as here expressed by Dylan is simultaneously "a doing and an undergoing."[11] Recall Wang Yang-ming's formulation of the unity of knowledge and action but now from the perspective of this rock-n-roll experience. Here knowledge is action and action is knowledge. What makes it possible? I believe it is the alternative state of being that Dylan has entered into. The contemporary Taoist master Ming Dao says this about knowledge in the contemporary world: "[K]nowing comes only when we have made the answers part of ourselves."[12] In other books I have suggested a way of knowing that I have come to call "felt intelligence."[13] A simple everyday experience is that of walking into a room. Immediately one senses vaguely but importantly that something is happening. Good professors have this feeling every time they enter the classroom. The feeling bears along with it some thing that expresses itself ever so slightly. That moment of perceptive understanding is what I mean by "felt intelligence."

The Chinese have known about this for a long time. They have a sacred book that has as its foundation this very feeling. It is the *Yijing*, and it revolves about feeling intelligently the "propensity of things."[14] We know that this sacred book develops a very sophisticated cosmology of change that employs the well-known forces of yin and yang to divine what is happening. One can use these tendencies to detect a sense of the mood and direction of specific situations. When things are at the moment of change, everything really is at stake. One has heard the following countless times: "The Chinese word for crisis is also the word for opportunity." And so it is. It is important to underscore the role of feeling in this experience. Feelings are at the root of human doing and knowing. From this primal level of awareness, knowing actions that inform the conscious state begin their rise and fall. Soul's inscape with its stress on integration and transformation is also rooted in this experience. This level of intelligence is felt throughout the body for the body is alive with awareness. Here the mind-body split is healed by reason of the knowing action characteristic of beings involved in their environmental situation.[15] It is this state of fusion that, like the "Dylan experience," demonstrates just how terribly abstract separated notions of the body and the mind really are. Furthermore, this act of felt intelligence appears to have an indefinite range among human beings. It can be solitary as when the hunter stalks her prey, or it can be communal as when the community dances together. Are you trying to locate where "body" and "mind" actually and concretely meet? Go to that region of continuous experience that expresses felt intelligence in action. And yin and yang are not absolutes, for yin means "not so yang," and yang means "not so yin."

But I am talking about "Soul." Given what this analysis has uncovered, Soul can now be understood as the concrete force that welds together the philosophically divided dimensions of human existence. Soul can do it with exquisite finesse or with clumsy surges of energy. One can fashion a law to express this dynamic act of healing dualistic philosophy: "Wherever and whenever a human being feels the sense of an alternative, then Soul expresses itself." Soul was there in the slave's hoot; Soul was there when Dylan sang; Soul was there when we stepped on the moon; and Soul was there when the baby was born. The omnipresence of Soul is a direct result of its inscape. Similarly, the joining of Souls in communal union is the direct outcome of Soul's involvement. Felt intelligence comes in individual forms and shapes but also in group expressions. Given our culture's commitment to rearing isolated individuals, this fertile soil of individual and communal creativity remains untended.

As a college professor I witness on a daily basis the results of these colonizing forces. Minds are dulled. Awareness barely stirs. Imagination is confined to situation comedies or tragedies or so-called reality shows. The damage done is exponentially enlarged by shopping channels that fixate awareness on isolated products. No depth and reach of continuity can affect minds so riveted by the daily repetition of "the same old, same old." Without links supplied by lived personal and communal experience, awareness cannot reach the level of tension required to provoke a sense of the alternative. There is no need for a "what else is there" if everything is continually served up for microwaving in our Souls. The entertained democracy sits back and watches the show.

The quality of our feeling for a genuine alternative is reduced to a minimum. Only information is passed around. It is somewhat grandly called "data," but it is what it is: facts and figures structured to demonstrate a point. Consciousness dwells entirely in "the Land of Is." Power point demonstrations spring up in the darkened spaces where university learning takes place. Who is awake? Who has dozed off? And what about those opened computer lids behind which our students hunker down. Do we really know what Johnny and Linda College are looking at as we catch a glimpse of them sitting way back there in the last row with their learning machines opened for business? Maybe they are really watching TV. And who could blame them when they are but two among the hundred or so students crammed into the classroom?

And what of that other place where Soul really lives: "The Land of Ought?" I am speaking of the world of values where the important is discussed, argued for and against, presented clearly, and linked up with everyday lives. I teach Plato's *Republic* to freshman students. I sense their admiration for the Spartans with their courage, discipline, and fierce loyalty. It is very much like the armed forces commercials that they see every day and every night on their TV screens. Now here is something they can connect with: athletic teams, contests of valor, survivor shows, and all that goes with the single-minded pursuit of honor. But what happens when they are shown that such ways of behavior have a dark side—that the very honor the Spartans seek is bestowed on them by others and that they then become enslaved to the approval of others? But it can become even worse. Morbidly connected to the approval and recognition of others, bravery gives birth to an inner uncertainty. Are they as good as the other? Are they better? Who shall decide their worth? A feel for the alternative begins to rise in different parts of the classroom. They sense that a culture built solely on honor has catastrophic costs—suspicion and envy enter the lives of the citizen.

Compared to the massive forces arranged to shape awareness in a single way, this example of a possible classroom lecture on a small part of Plato's *Republic* seems to be a pitiful counterforce. There really is a fearsome assault on our Souls carried out on a 24/7 time schedule. I recall once driving through New York City and looking up at the massive "projects" that housed the poor and the lower middle class. Inside almost every dimly lit apartment, a blue light glowed. It was the TV flickering images into the room as it announced the great values and dreams of the day. The sounds that accompanied the images were high-decibel noise that made thinking impossible. Conversation with one's family and friends was out of the question. Throughout the city and all across the country human beings were being systematically shut off from any feeling for the alternative. By reason of its inscape Soul is marked with the possibility of great energy and liveliness. Aristotle called it the "principle of life," and the Chinese still call it *"ch'i,"* the source of vitality. Feeling the sense of an alternative is the central channel through which Soul strengthens human growth. And yet the cultural drive for mass consumption and a single-minded vision of the good life seems to be a juggernaut that cannot be stopped.

Is there any counterweight to TV's 24/7 assault on our consciousness? One possible candidate is increasing the Soul's intensity of feeling. Some presence must challenge the deadening effect of addictive television viewing. Some expression must come to the fore that is equal to the images parading across the television screen. The prisoners in Plato's cave faced a similar dilemma. How were they to "stand up and turn around" so that they could experience the feeling of an alternative. Plato's description of this act uses the word *agon*. It is the source of our word "agony," but a far more menacing meaning lurks within the original Greek word. *Agon* is the technical term for the "death grip" used in Greek wrestling matches. A wrestler snapped his opponent's neck and what once faced forward now faced backward. In other words, he was dead. So the prisoner who escapes must suffer *agon*. He dies to his previous world of consciousness and undergoes *metanoia*, a change of awareness. Discussion of the consequences of this transformation of consciousness consumes the remainder of the *Republic*, a study that ends with a discussion of hell and various possibilities of rebirth.

In the end this feeling for the alternative that defines the conscious Soul marks out the primal meaning of Soul as experienced throughout the actual world. To seek the alternative is to be spontaneous; better yet, it is to express spontaneity. Where Soul is, there is a freshness that is a sign of novelty. Does our culture possess an expression so powerful that it can stand up to and reverse the ever-flickering "blue lights" of our televised culture? I suggest it resides in those disciplines in the humanities that echo Plato's concern for values that lead to the best life for all. We can take heart in the very real *fact* that the *values* of the human self are still in the making. The love of wisdom compels Soul to measure the right relation between *facts* and *values*. We have yet to become who we can be. Expression is the inscape of Soul, but expression that does not provoke involvement is not expression. What is required is eloquence, the subject of the next chapter.

4

ELOQUENCE ARISING

Art washes away from the soul the dust of every day.
—Pablo Picasso

In this chapter I argue that Soul at its most powerful transforms expression into "eloquence on the rise." Eloquence is best defined as that which gets the most out of the least. Eloquence draws no attention to itself and vanishes for the sake of the effect it achieves. The major aim of eloquence is the expression of value. Value is brought forth through the various forms of expression that a culture invents and identifies as important. In our day these forms of expression fall under the general term *media*. Today there are a multitude of media employed to capture the attention of Soul. Any media employed shares a single structure that provokes a genuine sense of the alternative.

Whitehead said: "All value is the outcome of limitation."[1] Our culture is mired in clichéd vulgarity. It seems as though sex, violence, and the grotesque display of wealth are the only themes that attract attention. Soul is expression, and its power to convey meaning is the vital concern of our time. The importance of Whitehead's words cannot be overstressed. What does it mean to make value dependent on limitation? Restraint appears to be the direct opposite of a culture whose slogan is "More." Limit's contribution to value lies in its power to express the fact that value is always an event and not a thing. It is to be experienced in a specific time and place. It comes and goes. It springs from a relevant past, expresses itself in a dominant present, and fades off into an unknown future. Value experienced as an event has a definite unity; otherwise vagueness would invade its very being, and it could never really express itself. To say that value has the unity of an event is to say that it has a definite specific form. Form's capacity to express value is dependent upon the value of the human Soul. Soul is therefore the chief contender in the cultural arena. The sense of an alternative required for restoring our culture's health depends upon choosing the right form to convey meanings. There are a multitude of forms in our contemporary world, and every sunrise seems to bring another. How are we to sort out the relevant form that will elegantly express the values we cherish? The thought of the American philosopher Charles S. Peirce is of direct importance in this struggle to express value through limit.

Peirce regarded every natural occurrence or event as a sign. Its very being is to be found in its mode of expression. So deep was Peirce's commitment to this philosophical view that he called Soul a "sign" and did so with great confidence:

> But are we shut up in a box of flesh and blood? When I communicate my thoughts to a friend with whom I am most in full sympathy . . . do I not live in his brain as well as in my own—literally? True my animal life is not there; but my soul, my feelings, thoughts, attention are. . . . If this be not so, a man is not a word, it is true, but something much poorer. There is a miserable . . . notion, according to which a man cannot be in two palaces at once; as though he were a *thing!* — A word may be in several places at once . . . because its essence is spiritual; and I believe that a man is no whit inferior to the word in this respect.[2]

Spontaneity is the sparkle of life. It breathes forth a freshness and vitality that marks the emergence of life. Without signs of life, human existence dries up, withers, and loses its verve. Energy disappears and is replaced with a sluggish repetitiveness. Peirce's semiotic theory begins with spontaneity. He calls it "firstness" for it is that which is indelibly there at the very beginning of Soul's work. But Soul does not rest there for it must develop through other stages to achieve its own rightful eloquence. But first there must be firstness. It is felt with stunning immediacy. Upon being expressed, it summons direct participation. It is its own originality.

As Peirce puts it: "[Stop] to think of it and it has flown. What the world was to Adam on the day he opened his eyes to it, before he had drawn any distinctions, or had become conscious of his own existence,—that is first, immediate, new imitative, original, spontaneous, free, vivid, conscious, evanescent. Only, remember that every description of it must be false to it."[3]

Freshness is also caught in the conversation between Mr. Deasy and Stephen Daedalus in the opening pages of *Ulysses*:

> —History, Stephen said, is a nightmare from which I am trying to awake.
> From the playfield the boys raised a shout. A whirring whistle: goal. What if that nightmare gave you a back kick?
> —The ways of the Creator are not our ways, Mr. Deasy said.
> All history moves toward one great goal, the manifestation of God.
> Stephen jerked his thumb towards the window, Saying:
> —That is God.
> Hooray! Ay! Whrrwhee!
> What, Mr. Deasy asked?
> A shout in the street, Stephen answered, shrugging his shoulders.[4]

The first lesson to be learned about eloquence is that it need not be a long, drawn out peroration. Here learned theology is cast aside for a fresh look at the Western God. Empty words, no matter how beautifully couched, are still vacant. The contemporary media knows nothing about firstness for it confuses it with gaining attention. The television show opens with a rape. The movie starts with a murder, and the news always headlines the sensational. As these repetitive attention grabbers grow stale, freshness subsides, and the citizens slouch back into their cushioned chairs.

False firstness leaves the viewer awaiting the next thrill. True freshness is in Peirce's semiotics, expressed by an icon—an icon is a likeness, a resemblance. It says much about our culture that the very word is now used to signify a 'one-of-its-kind,' a hero, an unmistakable expression of quality. So Alex Rodriguez is an icon, and so is Madonna, and all the while others struggle to push them off the pedestal. As foolish as these uses of the word are, they do manage to bring forth some of the real meaning of icon. For they suggest the first appearance of value in a realm where there was none. But false freshness only leads to more cultural staleness. An icon announces the unique and exceptional presence of an emergent quality. It does not, however, reach the level of full expression.

And what does firstness have to do with Soul as expression? At first it was only the Pentagon that taught us how to live in a world of acronyms, but now the entire culture—young, old, mercantile, educational, and healthy—lives in a world of alphabetic brevity. A new nomenclature has arisen. Each profession has its own reduced version of firstness. Higher education, which should know better, is often the most offensive. Business, industry and the military have long been leaders in this campaign to freeze thought in a display of consonants and vowels. Of course one cannot leave out the government, which is a prime source of this confusion. This new form of alphabetic brevity that now functions as actual words is an inevitable result of the speed factor that has taken over our lives. Email and its lingo, instant messaging, cell phones, and now twittering and on and on—we live in the world of 24/7 where it is impossible to catch one's breath. And let us not forget "multitasking."

In 1925 Alfred North Whitehead saw this coming and wrote of the professional man: "Then, almost suddenly, a pause occurred, and in its last twenty years the [last] century closed with one of the dullest stages of thought since the time of the First Crusade. It was an echo of the eighteenth century, lacking Voltaire and the reckless grace of the French aristocrats. The period was efficient, dull, and half-hearted. It celebrated the triumph of the professional man.[5]

We have had more than eighty years to develop this type of person. It must be said that we have succeeded beyond our wildest dreams. In my home institution, the professionals are grappling with "a hole in the budget" (caused by no faculty member, no student, no staff, no member of the support staff, and no member of the facilities management staff). It was solely maladministration at the top level of the university administration that brought about this crisis. Administrators recently announced with great gusto that a new plan would enable them to eliminate ninety *positions*. No one stopped to notice that ninety human beings occupied those positions. So Whitehead's "professional man" has mutated. The professional is no longer half-hearted. Corporate culture has replaced our universities as sanctuaries of free speech. Because by definition the corporate world has no heart, the professional is now a vital necessity. And, of course being indispensable, these professionals protect themselves very well.

We seem to have strayed far from the eloquence of Soul, but in fact we have not. The corruption of language, which is the heartbeat of these cultural transformations, does indeed feed the dis-ease of the

Soul. In fact, properly understood, such linguistic degeneracy brings us directly to the second level of Peirce's semiotics, secondness. Firstness by itself alerts us to value, but that value must secure a place in the world of actual expression. All actual real moments of firstness fade and are challenged by secondness. As a sign, secondness expresses the brutal clashes of experience that prove the mettle of the signs of firstness. Here we meet the index, the blunt, and the guaranteed. As the term *secondness* asserts, an index arises from firstness and points directly at a second moment that asserts a causal *relation* between the sign and the object signified. Where there is smoke there is fire. The astonishing spontaneity of firstness expressing all its freshness of value collides with the results of its arrival in the actual world. Outcomes and consequences, clear, direct, and immediate meet the innocence of firstness and challenge its results. Perhaps it was only the perfume of suggestiveness, or perhaps it was the emergence of a value that will have altered the future in very significant ways. Whatever the result of the particular case, the sign of secondness is the index of what is actually occurring in the world of continuing events. Peirce said: "[T]he second is precisely that which cannot be without the first. It meets us in such facts as Another, Relation, Compulsion, Effect, Dependence, Independence, Occurrence, Result."[6] A false secondness leads the world astray. Just as the felt tone of firstness is surprise, so also the feeling tone of secondness is compulsion. We are pulled along to see the world in a certain way. One can immediately foresee the danger implicit in a world of alphabetic brevity. There is no room for thought. Once an idea receives its alphabetic ordination, all questioning of its validity vanishes. One should say it more strongly: thought is banished and obedience demanded. In our culture it has become an indicative force pointing toward success. We 'will' do this, or we will 'not' do that. It is all about what people mean by the "school of hard knocks" and "the way things are." It is the presence of otherness in our lives and expresses the fact there are causes and conditions in our lives that may bring about "unfortunate but inevitable" consequences. It is expressed as an index because this level of reality points to the fact that process is not over yet. The surprise of what was first is met by the resistance of what is next. And Soul is thrown into the hurly-burly of concrete life. Without the force of indexical signs we are living in a dream world of our own fantasy. It is a bare judgment on a process that has not reached its conclusion. We halt at the collision between the value of firstness and the fact of secondness. We are left stymied, paralyzed, and stuck in a quagmire of suggestive values and recalcitrant facts. No eloquence can emerge from such a stalemate. Soul is thwarted in its drive toward integrated transformation. Something has to happen if Soul is to grow.

The expression that is Soul will proclaim itself when thirdness arrives. What is more, authentic eloquence now becomes a real possibility. Thirdness indicates that level of expression within which prior conflicts are resolved and genuinely full articulation is reached. A fully developed sign or symbol expresses the fact that a process has reached a level of stability or thirdness *and is able to express it as such*. It is the culmination of the reach for significance. Furthermore, this third, what can now be termed a "symbol" is understood as such by the community within which its meaning is recognized and shared. Expression has been housed in a sign that demands further interpretation as the community grows by working through continuous challenges. The symbol must be alive and it must have depth. When the symbols of our culture become habitual—that is to say, when they approach the level of generally recognized patterns of the real—then a quality of depth of meaning has been attained. Soul receives its full expression in thirdness and is present in the most intense way. Or to put it in terms of Peirce's semiotic theory: the symbol "is (not) so much a new meaning as a return to its original meaning."[7] Firstness has struggled with secondness, and together they have made a third. One plus two equals three.

There are deep resonances of this structure of development in the history of philosophy and psychology. One thinks immediately of the "hard labor" of Hegel's concept in attaining its completion as a full expression of spirit. One is also reminded of Freud's three stages of psychological development—oral, anal, and genital. And many others could be mentioned. But my point is that the Soul has its own struggles in achieving mature expression. In fact, I argue that what is generally called "character" is the attainment of full expression by the Soul. What is not to be missed in this journey of Soul is the important role played by the community in assisting its growth. Firstness is its 'inscape.' Secondness is 'involvement.' Thirdness is the intelligent feeling of an alternative that expresses fully Soul's character in its distinct humanity. We see now why the whispered slave 'hoot' is so expressive for it is simultaneously an original, a protest, and a symbol of community.

This brings us to an examination of the method underlying this effort to track the rise of eloquence. The rise of eloquence is an aesthetic achievement for it directly experiences feeling and seizes it in an initial expression. It then moves through opposition in a way that demands enlargement of meaning. Finally through its adoption by a human community, it achieves fullness of expression. Aesthetics originates in a desire for quality of expression. It also is the way in which we can become philosophically aware of feelings, their import, and their structure. What grounds aesthetics as a method is its understanding of contrast. Contrast is a way to have identity and difference together. It has other names. It can be called "harmony." It can be called "integration." It can also be understood as a potential answer to the problem of the one and the many. The structure of contrast brings together two grounds: a ground for unity and a ground for diversity. The ground for unity mediates the diversity inherent in the situation, problem, or opportunity facing Soul. The ground for diversity differentiates the various components involved in the situation, problem, or opportunity. Without diversity a shallow sameness could masquerade as a genuinely eloquent wholeness of expression. Without unity expression would drift away into meaningless items disconnected from the situation, problem, or opportunity. The first solution offers Soulless experience; the second, a heap of sorites unrelated to Soulful experience.

What contrast achieves is what Soul really needs: a way to have motion and rest, life and peace. Here we are trenching on Plato's turf: "The Stranger [replies:] The philosopher—the person who values these things the most—absolutely has to refuse to accept the claim that everything is at rest, either from the defenders of *the one* or the friends of the many forms. In addition he has to refuse to listen to people who say that which is changes in every way. He has to be like the child begging for 'both' and say that *that which is*—everything—comprises both *the unchanging* and *that which changes*."[8]

Just how does contrast give the child what she wants? Contrast enables difference to work under a sheltering identity. As enriched signs emerge as modes of expression, Soul receives the food it needs to rise to the level of eloquence.

Western civilization is not well suited to provide the safe haven needed to foster and nourish differences. Our history emphasizes individual assertion that often treads on others to win its place in the sun. The very word *win* speaks volumes about the competitiveness that so often underlies Western lifestyles. Nevertheless, there is also Plato's insight as expressed in the *Timaeus* where he calls the demiurge (read reason) the "foster mother" or "nurse" of all becoming. Mothers and nurses are caregivers, not forces that assault the world. Still, Plato's remark quickly dropped out of sight when the scientific revolution and its technological tools came to occupy the center of Western culture.

One of Hegel's great achievements is to restore to importance the sense of the alternative that allows expression to resurrect dead forms of life through reason's continuing effort to express the thing itself (*die*

Sache Selbst) as history demands ever more effective manifestations of Spirit's meaning.⁹ I believe his use of expressions such as "The Good Friday of Reason" and its crucifixion on Golgotha are much more than a dramatic recourse to New Testament images. The concreteness of the scenes themselves can only be felt by the individual Soul (firstness), then by lifting up that feeling by understanding its historical situation (secondness), and finally by being expressed in the community's participation in its liturgical expression (thirdness), the meaning of Hegel's cultural form receives full expression. Once more Soul does its work through expression that begins as a private moment, then meets opposition, and finally becomes a full expression through the presence of a community of witnesses.

Soul is not confined to Western philosophy. Thankfully comparative philosophy has recently begun to take its rightful place among the many forms of philosophical efforts. Indeed, references to Asian wisdom have become more and more important as human beings grapple with the problems brought on by an increasingly globalized civilization.¹⁰ Thus we can add to the philosophical resources reminding us of the reality of Soul the expressions of the Dao in Chinese philosophy. Daoism stresses the importance of nonassertion as a fundamental attitude toward the events of life. It regards aggressive stances as futile since antagonism in a world built up through relations defeats itself. Its ancient classic the *Tao Te Ching* continually reminds us to never use force. In addition we have the constant Confucian admonitions to never do to another what one would not have done to one's self. I could prolong the list, but the name *Gandhi* is enough to persuade us that welcoming difference is the high road to peace. *Satyagraha* was Gandhi's ultimate means to free his country from British oppression. *Satyagraha* means "Soul Force."

Wherein lies this Soul power? The burden of my argument is that Soul is expression. One final example of Asian wisdom that provides additional confirmation for this hypothesis is the Chinese tradition of living up to one's word. Not to live up to one's word is to betray Soul's eloquence and thereby bring down the foundations of human association. Eloquence has been employed as a paradigmatic expression of Whitehead's theory of truthful beauty. Touched upon earlier in this chapter, it now demands a more complete discussion if the concept of 'Soul as expression' is to be humanly useful. This is especially true in an age dominated by the clichés of deconstruction. Catch phrases such as "the fading of the subject," the "sliding of the object under the signifier," the implacable presence of "*difference*" in human speech and writing, the "instability" of meaning, the substitution of "the text" for the book, and even its "disappearance," only serve to prevent rigorous systematic thinking. Peirce's understanding of semiotics is a far more trustworthy guide to the mysteries of expression than the self-referential portrait of language invented by Saussure and put to work in deconstruction's effort to enfeeble and undermine cultural values. How such thinking can serve the interests of any multicultural program of study is beyond my understanding. In fact, it contradicts itself since no expression is stable enough to carry reliable expression and meaning.

To understand Whitehead's insistence on the significance of truthful beauty it is necessary first of all to grasp its various components:

> There is a background that shapes the values emerging from the experience.
> There are the strong individualities that find their place within the complex of values.
> There is a background that both shelters and highlights the distinctive character of these individuals.
> There is a foreground that brings together the various characters even as it preserves their unique qualities.

These ways of bringing identity and difference together are simply the reconstruction of what earlier has been called a "contrast." Furthermore understood as a gestalt, the structure protects the diversities, qualifies them as appropriate parts of the whole, and, when both beautiful and true, lifts them to a more intense level of expression. In so doing the reach and depth of experience receive an exponential expansion. In fact, when truthful beauty is functioning as it should, it then lays open for Soul depths of experience that "lie below the stale presuppositions of verbal thought."[11] This is Soul at its best for it is expressing creativity so deep in the womb of worldly experience that words fail and other means of expression must be sought. The arts in all their forms now come into play and enter the experiential domain of Soul. Even silence itself, as Samuel Beckett has shown, can be a suitable form of expression. This is why poetry, music, song, painting, and the other arts stir the Soul. We are dealing with a "Truth of Feeling."[12]

Whether this unification of experience is called a "gestalt," a "contrast," a "harmony," or an "integration," the fundamental quality sought by Soul in its creative process is eloquence. The question that remains at the end of this part of the reconstruction of the meaning of Soul is *what is eloquence?* Two qualities have so far been examined, poise and elegance. When they are brought together in human action *they express eloquence of Soul.* Poise rests on the tone of awareness achieved in the midst of difficulties and is the fruit of a sense of an alternative. Where some humans might lose their head, the person of poise holds steady and feels each of the possibilities resident in the situation at hand. There is no necessary need for force, and oftentimes words are useless. So poise is primarily a manifestation of restraint. It senses the vector of events and deploys it to resolve conflicted feelings. Elegance is the measure of effort used to resolve the discord festering within life's conflicts. Elegance does not exhaust itself with the unnecessary. It goes right to the heart of the matter at hand and as it was defined before "does the most with the least."

Eloquence need not require words, nor does it demand action. It can be the power of absolute silence. Or it can be the refusal to contend. Recall the legendary maxim whose history is buried in the mists of Zen lore: "hurl the fireball of *Mu*."[13] The lucidity characteristic of genuine eloquence lights up the dim corners of the fields of strife where solutions and even seemingly magical solutions are hidden away. Recall the eloquence Deng Shao Ping when faced with the political and social turmoil brought about by his attempt to transform the Chinese economy. Attacked on all sides for all sorts of reasons, he simply said, "Who cares what color the cat is as long as long as it catches the mouse." Many mistake this remark for mere cleverness. But rice is the staple food of China, and a mouse loves rice. Deng was speaking with direct elegance to the heartmind of the people.

These references to Asian culture mark out a difference noted before between Western recourse to force and Eastern reticence and restraint. There is nothing eloquent in the way in which George Bush began his war on Iraq. We all recall "shock and awe." Neither poise nor elegance is expressed in the rubble left behind. There is, however, an alternative strain of thought in Western culture. Beginning with Parmenides and expressed most eloquently by Plato and Plotinus the limit expressed by form is the very intelligibility of reality. To know the real is to know its determinateness. Some two thousand years later, Whitehead in attempting to fashion a new metaphysics for the modern world of atomic events and processes said the following: "How are we to characterize the something which thus emerges?. . . . [W]e see at once that the element of value, of being an end in itself, of being something which is for its own sake, must not be omitted in any description of an event as the most concrete something. 'Value' is the word I use for the intrinsic reality of an event . . . But there is no such thing as mere value. Value is the outcome of limitation."[14]

The decisive word is "limitation." Its opposite is excess or lack. Limitation, value, and intelligibility form a triad of themes that taken together express the importance of living a significant life. The key to fostering the rise of eloquence in the Soul is adding symbolic transmission to elegance and poise. By symbolic transmission I mean the various ways in which cultures express those general ideas which are the bedrock of their values. It is precisely at this point that poise and elegance can help to lift up limitation to the level of eloquent expression. It is also precisely at this point that our culture with its exaggerated claims of superiority stands in the way of authentic human growth and development. There is something truly strange about our culture's proud expressions of achievement and its attachment to alphabetic brevity as its primary symbolic mode of communication. We boast that we multitask and celebrate that tomorrow is already here even as the sun has yet to set on the present day.

Haste, speed, and alacrity are the signs that govern our culture. The drive to produce more and more in less and less time has become a common behavioral pattern. In some sense of course it is promoted by corporate capitalism's drive for profit, which demands a significant compression of the time labor needs to turn out its products. But there is something much more bizarre in this obsession to quicken the tempo of human life. Consider the phenomenon of email, focus on the incessant use of cell phones, pay attention to the inattention fostered by the use of ipods, and observe how humans cut each other out of their spatial and temporal lives. Faster and faster go our personal worlds. Then add to this single-minded individualism the mantra of the age, "More." Here indeed is a witches' brew calculated to stamp out eloquence as a real factor in human culture. At its heart this contemporary phenomenon is a direct challenge to the need for limit. Recall that limit is the ground of the emergence of the real. Without limit there is no form. Without form there is no intelligibility. Without knowledge there can be no decisive choice for the better rather than the worse. This is not the lament of an "old timer" who has been shoved aside in the race for glory, fame, and fortune. It is simply a stark observation of the ways in which our culture has turned against the possibility of the growth of eloquence. Buried within this cultural development is the "Soullessness" so many lost Souls feel is their lot in life.[15]

There is truly a worrisome irony expressed in this union of the "more" with the personal isolation brought about by the ipod and the communal culture of the e-world. Even the exuberance that attaches itself to cell phone activity is momentary. We are inducted more and more in the sealed off isolation caused by the advance of technical devices; but at the very same time our communal world expands exponentially as more and more 'advanced' devices are created. Those who use them often call them, "just more bells and whistles," but they signal actual increases in these instruments of communication. In sum, the detachment between the personal and the communal has taken on a much more sinister form. I ask the reader to recall the blue-toned, video-soaked living rooms of the impoverished.

So we have grown new eyes and new ears. What do they see? What do they hear? What will they see? What will they hear? Here is where the power of imagination ought to come into play. Imagination is not just a fantasy; rather as Kant points out it provides the indispensable prelude to intelligent knowing as well as the original sign of Soul in action.[16] Murray Code in his recent *Process, Reality, and the Power of Symbols* has provided a devastating analysis of just how this loss of living communication saps our culture of life, and then hands it over to forces utterly opposed to anything that threatens the routine business of living a human life.[17] The surprising, the unexpected and the novel are looked upon as adversaries to be suppressed if our corporate life is to continue. Similarly, Ralph Pred's extraordinary analysis of consciousness from a Whiteheadian point of view directly challenges the materials of philosophers such as John Searle and demonstrates just how much living and intense value slip out of such only partially understood nets of intentionality.[18] What ties these two recent studies together is the way in which both authors from different points of view protest against the loss of the quickness of life, which is the very touchstone of lived experience. In place of these invigorating moments of flashes of insight we are only offered more of the same. There is a great but hidden truth in our youngest children's frequent lament that contemporary experience is "boring, boring, boring."

So what are we to do with these new eyes and ears? The answer lies in the realm of meaning. The most straightforward definition of meaning is that it is the way in which a difference is registered. In a process world meaning is therefore an ever-shifting set of symbols that express eloquently or inadequately the novelty emerging in various situations. Now the range of symbolic efficacy is wide and varied. It can extend from zero intensity to previously unheard evocative eloquence. Or to put it into a more concrete cultural formula: meaning, symbolically expressed, can run the gamut from stunning eloquence to the endless repetition of previous states of being that are only slightly altered by the an almost indiscernible temporal difference. As we have come to express it (not so eloquently, but with a certain brute force) "same old, same old." But this symbolic register is precisely what a driven capitalist society desires. It sees routine as its most valuable asset and the creative as a threat. And this attitude does not confine itself to the market place. It can be seen in the endless sequels that follow hit movies. It is also expressed by educational institutions that for the sake of simplicity run the same courses over and over again for the sake of disciplinary integrity.

My mention of eyes and ears was deliberate for the entire human body is a field of expression. Eloquence is not restricted to language. Watch a superb athlete performing her sport. In the end there may not be that much difference between *self* and *Soul* as connotative words. I have chosen Soul so as to resurrect what has become in our culture a 'dead' word. Throughout her extraordinary career as a psychoanalyst Karen Horney had always been at pains to distinguish between the neurotic self and the real self. It is the neurotic self that lacks wholeheartedness due to the conflicts embedded in the Soul. The 'real self' on the other and is described this way by Horney:

> [W]hat I mean here is perhaps best indicated by William James' concept of the 'real self' as distinguished from the material or social self. In simple terms it is what I really feel, what I really want, what I really believe. What I really decide. It is, or should be, the most alive center of psychic life. It is this psychic center to which the appeal is made in analytical work. In every neurosis its scope and its aliveness are decreased, for genuine self-regard, native dignity, and initiative, the capacity to take responsibility for one's life, and like factors that account for the development of the self have always been battered.[19]

For the Greeks *psyche* meant life in the sense of movement, growth and what in general we call "quickness." Horney's understanding of what she calls the "Neurotic Personality of Our Time"[20] brings this study full circle back to the first chapter where the inscape of Soul was largely derived from Plato's concept of the Soul. Also Whitehead's reliance on Plato's *Timaeus* to describe the general features of Soul needs to be kept firmly in mind.[21] Finally the recent work of Murray Code may be read as one long appeal to restore the "quicknesses" of our lives in the face of the onslaught of factors arrayed to numb our psychic being.[22] The function of imagination is to bring forth symbols that will enliven (quicken) our sense of participation in a real world whose values are steadily eroded by a culture that seeks security above all else and depends on a misplaced reliance on the power of science and its offspring technology to keep the "same old, same old" running in place with the process that is the actual reality of our lives.

What is at stake in this cultural malaise is the place afforded to genuine creativity. The doctrine of harmony previously described unites both strong individuality and synthetic power. In our day celebrity takes the place of individuality, and only iconic display merits media attention. One can even become famous by becoming famous. What one is famous for does not matter as long as the deed, lifestyle can be made prominent and even legendary. Celebrities replace heroes and our democracy becomes solely interested in and satisfied by entertainment. As a result the unity of foreground and background is shattered and no flash of genuine creative insight can express itself. What is simply good in itself is no longer acknowledged. Hegel is all too right when he unites desire and reason as the first step toward self-consciousness. It is within this alliance between feeling and intelligence that human self-consciousness becomes possible. But one last component must be added. Without recognition, signs give up the ghost and Soul dries up. This is why cultural excellence is so important. Where there is no genuine response possible, there eloquence fades. And the rest, as it is said, is silence. Inscape needs involvement, and the feeling of an alternative is brought to concrete life through expression. Plato's doctrine of Eros as the foundation of knowing teaches the same lesson. In the *Symposium* Diotima tells Socrates that love is neither a god nor a human but a messenger that grounds community.[23] *Koinonia* demands recognition.

A process universe demands a dizzying array of symbols to make thought effective and Soul alive. What troubles us is the very real suspicion that our culture has neither width nor depth. As a result no eloquence emerges, and Soul dies. How can it be than more than four thousand American soldiers die and countless Iraqis are killed and the majority of Americans go shopping? Soul death stalks the land, and the Four Horsemen of the *Apocalypse*—Famine, Plague, War, and Death—ride the planet. What can restore a sense of the liveliness of our existence is a full-bodied array of resources for expression, recognition, and community life. Earlier I warned against "forgetting the body" even as we searched for Soul growth. Among Whitehead's many great contributions to philosophy is the reconstruction of the experiential process underlying human perception. First, he insists upon perception as an act and not a passive reception of sense data. Second, he demonstrates how the human body in its parts and in its whole is the origin and the ground of our entrée into the external world. This is what he means by the terms *prehension* and *causal efficacy*. We are already part of the world for the very acts of our being take place within the world. Spectator knowledge is a high abstraction that does not deliver the kind of depth and reach needed for expressive eloquence. Without such qualities Soul drifts back into a morbid existence scarcely noticed by the human community. There are three basic environmental communities that Soul can feel as springs of value: the biological, the environmental and the cultural. Of course in human experience they are mostly interfused. What counts is the way in which Soul grasps these sources of nourishment. Further what also counts are the resources stored up from the past and made available to Soul. Thus Soul and various environments interlock to express what is of significance. In sum, without an effective past, a living present, and an available future the expressive tone of Soul cannot be felt.

Symbolic reference (Whitehead's term for the spiritual dimension of communication in every act of perception) is the actual world as most intensely felt and most intensely expressed. Signs are the lifeblood of a vibrant Soul. The lesson for the possibility of eloquence arising should now be clear—the mingling of affective and reasonable signs is the necessary condition for reclaiming for Soul its positive presence in our world. Whether this is an actual possibility at the present remains an open question. Cultural therapeutics has always been part of philosophy's obligations. The fact that the well of expression appears to have run dry does not remove that responsibility. We wait to see what the future will bring. Eliot's fisherman knows this: "I sit upon the shore fishing with the dry land behind me."[24]

5

ETERNAL AND TEMPORAL CONTRASTS

> I still do not quite understand why so many people have difficulty with the idea of eternity, except that their imagination must be glued to temporal analogies.
>
> —Robert Neville, *Eternity and Time's Flow*

As a philosopher seeking to communicate with my fellow human beings, I often feel that I must sail between Scylla and Charybdis. The abstract niceties of my subject matter can pull me in the direction of an almost incomprehensible abstractness (what Joyce called "the true scholastic stink"). Or I can vulgarize the subject matter by seeking to communicate through a bad simplicity (and thereby don the mantle of the new age guru who really does not know what she is talking about). Like Ulysses, I now strap myself to the mast and struggle against the siren songs of both temptations. In what follows I lean heavily on the pioneering work of Robert Neville who in both *Eternity and Time's Flow*[1] and *Symbols of Jesus* provides a lucid and fully understandable explanation of the dynamic relation between eternity and time. I propose to discuss the fact that time and eternity comprise one subject and not two. Furthermore, we must understand the fact that both eternity and time are bound together in mutual dynamic contrastive contact.

Without some reference to eternity time makes no sense, and without some reference to time eternity is empty. If time has no relation to eternity then what happens to all the dynamics we are accustomed to attribute to time: becoming, dynamism, creativity, novelty, growth, and advance? Time is not self-explanatory because its flow is not self-explanatory. The past does not explain itself. Where did it come from? Another past: but that creates a vicious circle. The present: where does it come from? The past: but the past has already gone. The future: but it is not yet. Therefore without some sense of the connection between time and eternity, time is rendered philosophically meaningless. Eternity is to be understood as both cause and source of time. If either side of the union of time and eternity is dismissed, then all sorts of halftruths emerge and are encouraged by certain philosophical systems. I am thinking of the incurable *angst* of extreme forms of existentialism on the one hand and the fierce use of delusional *maya* as expressed in extreme forms of Vedanta. Everything hinges on the correct understanding of the quality and meanings of the relations between eternity and time. To begin, these are the four points that shape Neville's argument in *Eternity and Time's Flow*:

The first is that "time and eternity" make one topic, not two.

> The second concerns time itself: time can be understood to flow only as contained within the ontological context of eternity. . . . The togetherness of the temporal modes such that time flows, is the true meaning of eternity.
> The third thesis concerns God: as the context for time's flow, eternity is to be understood according to a theory of divine creation. That is, the togetherness of the temporal modes in which time's flow consists is created *ex nihilo* by an eternal ontological act. . . .
> The fourth thesis, of most practical interest for human religious sensibility, is that personal immortality is eternal and participates in the divine life.[2]

Time is not eternal, and eternity is not temporal, but somehow they share a relation. This means that some form of togetherness is at work in the contrast between eternity and time. The kind of struggle going on is forever hidden to us mortals for it began as a singular divine creative act that was done from nothing. All this is to say that before creation we have no idea whatsoever of the divine. This bears repeating: before creation there was nothing for us mortals to know. This creative act is the *singular* eternal act that is the source of the modes of time that we experience. We experience time as having three temporal modes—past, present, and future—and it is because of these modes that we experience time *as flow*.

The term *mode* is not temporal for it is a form and not temporal. A form breathes fire into the cosmos, and something must be identified as the source of that blaze of activity. *That something is the divine life.* Therefore, as Neville puts it:

> Time in Things, Things in Eternity
> Things in Time, Time in Eternity.[3]

Understanding these relations will make clear the shift in meanings that occurs when time's flow and eternity are contrasted. First of all, note that time and eternity are opposites. If they are together then there must be an ontological context of mutual relevance. This context is what human beings have historically called "God." Furthermore given the meaning of time, there must also be a source for its creation that is outside time. Time by itself is not self-explanatory. Why? Because the past is different from the present and the future, the present is different from the past and the future, and the future is different from the past and the present. Each actual temporal zone is opposed to the other two. If this did not happen, then the meaning of time would collapse for time is to be understood as the happening of a difference. By themselves each actual past, each actual present, and each actual future is by definition unable to hold the relevant other two actual time zones together. Their opposition is fundamental to their meanings, and therefore we cannot use it to account for the flow of the actual past into the actual present and the actual future, the flow of the actual present out of the relevant actual past and into the relevant actual future, and the flow of the future as continuing the dimensions of the relevant actual past and the relevant actual present. *Flow*, the very definition of time, remains unaccounted for by the constituent dimensions of temporality itself. We must look for the reason for temporal flow outside the actual time flow itself.

Where do we look? The only reasonable place has to be eternity, but as seen earlier there is no time in eternity. What is in eternity are the modes (or forms) of time and not time itself. God, understood now as the ontological context of mutual relevance, is the singular creator *ex nihilo* of the modes of time past, time present, and time future. Singular here means unique and *once and for all*. God is always the actual context of mutual relevance that allows time to flow. God is there all the time because God as eternal creator is not in time. God is the singular creative context of mutual relevance that provides for the togetherness of time's flow from out of a past to a present and toward the future.

"Time in things" signifies that all things in the temporal world have as their essential feature time itself. The everyday world is thick with time. The existence of each thing is marked by a density as well as a beginning, duration, and end. Aristotle stressed becoming; Whitehead stressed the "perpetually perishing." Beginnings, durations, and endings sum up the outstanding features of the temporal world.

"Things in eternity" are bereft of these actual time zones. There is no time in eternity. However, each thing has already achieved an identity through the sway of time, and this identity is its achieved value. Time as value being achieved is always separated as past value achieved, present value being achieved, and future value to be achieved. This is what accounts for the rhythmic vibrations so important in Chinese and Indian philosophies. Rhythm is repetition with a difference, and as such there is always a static interruption in the temporal realm. We know this instinctively and use it to compose our approach to temporal existence. There is nothing sillier than teenagers acting like their elders unless it is an elder acting like a teenager. The question remains, where is the *flow* of time? The answer is in eternity. To grasp this is also to grasp the irreducible dynamism of eternity for "only in eternity is the dynamism of change significant."[4] To think of eternity as that place where nothing ever changes and all is perfect and without movement is to miss entirely the dynamic quality of eternal life. "Things in eternity" expresses this seeming paradox: "Time does not flow within time but within eternity."[5]

"Things in time" raises the question of personal identity. An answer frequently given is that the meaning of personal identity is to be found in the way a continuous thread of causes can be considered as continuous throughout a lifetime. This means that death is the end of the person, but as has been seen, time in and of itself cannot account for the flow of a person's life. That flow is grounded in eternity, and it therefore makes good philosophical sense to say that a person's identity is a togetherness whose full reality can only be had in eternity. Furthermore, this eternal personal reality must be true to the person's temporal life. It must in other words contain "within it the movement of the changing present."[6] Energy, dynamism, and liveliness are therefore to be experienced in eternity.

"Time in eternity" means that eternity houses time so that it can flow, but the eternal house of time is a mode and not a temporal event. Therefore time in eternity signifies the active presence of all the dimensions of time. Consequently, the modes of time are active in eternity because it is only outside time that time's flow can be fully understood. This flow is manifestly active; otherwise, it would not flow. The value of time's past, present, and future can only be adequately expressed in eternity. One consequence of this is that we can understand how it makes sense to say that eternity is God's life. The presence of God as the ontological context of mutual relevance demands that the flow of temporal life be fully realized in the divine eternal presence. This also implies that human beings can live within the divine life as their home. So the house of eternity is the home of humanity. Time and eternity are forever held in a contrast.

Previously I struggled to describe the ways in which contrasts lead to the most intense experiences possible. Think now of the immense intensity of feeling felt by those who live within the life of divinity. If eternity and time and their relationship are properly understood, words must fail to express the feeling tone of harmony held together by God's power. Remember a contrast holds identity and difference together. The preceding was an attempt to describe and illuminate the various ways in which the activity of the contrast between eternity and time play out. What contrast gives is what I have called a "feeling for the alternative." This is what constitutes the contours of the togetherness of the divine and the human. Forever experiencing alternatives is not unlike looking at a kaleidoscope. Eternity is no dull experience. It is a dynamic field that is essentially ineffable. When mystics try to describe their experiences, they invariably express their failure to describe what happened. But Soul is expression.

We have reached an undeniable impasse. Soul is an act of expression, and yet it fails when it experiences that which is its most intense possible experience. One is tempted to say, "Is this any way to live?" At this point it is useful to recall the famous opening of the *Tao Te Ching*:

> Tao called Tao is not Tao
> Names can name no lasting names
>
> Nameless: the origin of heaven and earth
> Naming: the mother of ten thousand things.
>
> Empty of desire, perceive mystery
> Filled with desire, perceive manifestations.
>
> These have the same source, but different names.
> Call them both deep—

> Deep and again deep:
> The gateway to all mystery.[7]

By describing God "The ontological context of mutual togetherness," Neville gives us an extremely abstract picture of God. To some that might be chilling, but consider the advantages. All cultures may now fill in that abstraction with their own actual and concrete traditions. That is a great service to those who wish to have a real conversation about God that avoids on the one hand shallow agreements and on the other dogmatic assertions, as the first poem in the *Tao Te Jing* says, "the gateway to all mysteries." Still: this most ancient text tells us that Tao cannot be expressed. But if Soul is expression, does not Soul run into a brick wall? After all the conceptual labor spent by Neville and us in seeking to understand his theory, this seems like a most disappointing outcome. There is however a way out of this impasse.

Tao may remain hidden in terms of verbal expression, but it is livable. The rest of the *Tao Te Ching* tells us how to live out this situation. Soul expresses itself by how it lives. If we call to mind the inscape of Soul as well as its involvement in the world we see how Soul's endowment is precisely what is needed in order to live Tao or any other ultimate realities professed by the human race. To review: Soul's inscape (chapter 1) allows for the creative transformation of situations and also intensity of feeling. Soul is subjective in the sense that it is always *my* experience that carries the weight of expression. The quality of Soul's unified integration of experiences is the measure of its spirituality. As we have learned through hard, cruel, and sorrowful experiences, not all spiritualities are equal. Soul's involvement in the world and the manner in which its conduct expresses Soul's posture toward otherness (chapter 2) leads to normative judgments as to better or worse and even good and evil. This stance is determined by the width and depth of its feeling for alternatives (chapter 3). This temporal openness is determined by Soul's relation to the eternal. In turn the rising of its eloquence (chapter 4) is a concrete act of expression. This act is the measure of the quality of its achieved harmony of the temporal and the eternal.

Susanne Langer calls the third part of the first volume of her masterwork on the mysteries of the mind's connection to human feeling "*Natura Naturans*." In a most elegant philosophical text she calls attention to the primacy of the "act":

> It is with the concept of the act that I am approaching living form in nature, only to find it exemplified there at all

levels of simplicity or complexity, in concatenations and in hierarchies, presenting many aspects and relationships that permit analysis, construction and special investigation. The act concept is a fecund and elastic concept. . . . Such events arise where there is a fairly constant movement going on. They normally show . . . [an] intensification of a distinguishable dynamic pattern, then reach a point at which the pattern changes, whereupon the movement subsides. That point of general change is the consummation of the act. The consequent phase, the conclusion or cadence, is the most variable aspect of the total process.[8]

Exchange "expression" for "act," and you have a summary of what I have been saying throughout this volume. Equally intriguing is her invocation of Spinoza's Latin term for nature (*Natura Naturans*) in the process of expression.[9] I cite Whitehead in defense of what I am about to suggest and call to mind his method of composing differences through the adjustment of concepts in other philosophers' major systematic works. Neither Lao-Tse, nor Neville nor Langer nor Spinoza would completely agree with my impending use of his or her thought.[10] My aim is to put some flesh and blood on the dry bones of the foregoing abstract analysis of eternity, time, and the concept of the act of expression.[11] I believe there is much value in this way of reading philosophers. Quite obviously, this is my work, and any objection should be directed at my ideas and not those of these eminent philosophers.

This is Spinoza's definition of eternity: "By eternity I mean existence itself, insofar as it is conceived as necessarily following solely from the definition of an eternal thing. . . . [It] cannot be explicated through duration or time, even if the duration be conceived as without beginning or end."[12] This is in direct accord with Neville's understanding of eternity as timeless. There is, of course, a significant difference between Spinoza and Neville on many issues. Certainly, Neville would not concur with Spinoza's idea of freedom as being what you have to be.[13] My use of Spinoza centers on his idea of the "*Liber*," or free Soul. To grasp its central place in the recovery of Soul we must understand in an unavoidably compressed fashion, the general structure and intent of the *Ethics*. A major aim of the *Ethics* is to make understandable and useful for the Soul the experience of Unity. Togetherness, the One and the Many, and solidarity are among the ultimate notions embedded in the meaning of unity. Unity is not a thing but an event characterized by the integration of experienced relations. Spinoza's substance is the dynamic process whereby the totality of that which is expresses itself as the indwelling cause of the becoming and the perishing of its particular parts. This metaphysics demands that the whole be regarded as simple and the parts complex. Though this completely overturned the then reigning Cartesian point of view, it was not sufficient to alter the course of materialistic interpretations of nature. Even today scientific materialism continues to follow Descartes' advice in this matter. We build cyclotrons and brain imaging machines to continue the search for the fundamental particles and the most minute neurons and axons in the brain. Parts are basic, primary, and fundamental; the whole is secondary and awaits the discovery of the elementary parts. The whole is to be built later out of the discovery of the constituent parts.[14] Spinoza reverses this way of looking at the world and insists through his logic of wholes and parts that there can be only one substance or fully real entity. All else is a relation emerging from the indestructible unity and activity of substance. Each particular entity has its identity by reason of its relation to others and ultimately by reason of the tone and quality of its relation to substance. There are no independent realities. Spinoza asks us to enter a world of verbs and adverbs rather than nouns and adjectives. Identity is discovered by the relations between things, not the things themselves. Like it or not this means that a finite mind cannot *intellectually* grasp the concrete whole of which it is a part. This does not say that we cannot *experience* the significance of the whole or act in accord with it. In other words our emotional life (experiences) and our conduct (ethics) must be understood as part of this active unity. Substance, God, or Nature is the source from which we set out to think. It is also the source to which we must refer our feelings and actions so as to comprehend their value.

    The unity of reality is to be understood as power where this term means the power to express. Reality is wholly verbal: it is always *be-ing* and this being is always an expression. There are no gaps or spots of nonbeing since the universe itself is power—the total, internally related togetherness of everything that was, is, and will be.

    As soon as human beings from infancy to their death enter this world of unity, they experience *involvement*. The value of this involvement is what human emotions are all about. Our feelings register the pitch, tone, and harmonic quality of our involvement with unity.[15] Feelings are indicators of the level of our relation as *part in*, *of*, *to*, and *with* the whole. Therefore Spinoza's theory of the emotions is not an attempt to rationalize away or intellectually eliminate our feelings. Emotions are forces. But ideas are also forces insofar as they *affirm* truth. To affirm an idea as true and to feel a feeling as a force is to come to understand the battlefield upon which Soul's happiness is won or lost. In sum, Spinoza's first work, *de Intellectus Emendatione,* is not as existing translations would have it a treatise on "The Improvement of the Understanding" or the "Correction of the Mind." Rather it ought to be translated as "The Healing of the Mind." Healing means the restoration to wholeness and wholeness foretells unity as the ultimate significance of the involvement binding Souls to each other, God or Nature.

Who is the Liber or Free Soul? The answer is a Soul that experiences *scientia intuitiva* and has thereby grasped the fundamental features of our emotional life. While it is true that feelings are a form of human bondage, it is not the case that the absence of feelings is the form of Soul's liberation. What is required is the transformation of our feelings from passive motives for action to active ways of being. When an emotion is understood, it does not necessarily change. Change takes place when Soul sees into (*intuitiva*) the concrete level of involvement entailed in a feeling. Once this knowledge (*scientia*) is experienced, Soul is transformed because Soul is what it knows. It is not that Soul *does* anything: it is rather that Soul *becomes* something else; that is to say, Soul is really different due to the level of its involvement. Such is the affirmative power of an idea when it truly knows an emotion.

This is a difficult point. To understand it more clearly, let us examine the three primary emotions—desire, joy, and sadness. Their names and definitions signal the particular ways Soul orientates itself toward unity. These emotions are first of all and for the most part not private subjective states but indicators of unity with all of reality or the lack thereof. Desire, joy, and sadness are primary in the sense that all other emotions spring from them. Desire is "the effort (*conatus*) by which each thing endeavors to persevere in its own being but this effort is the actual essence of the thing itself."[16] Conatus is therefore Soul in its active inscape. From this conatus and its desire to express (or to be), there arises the possibility of expressing (or being) more or less. This follows from the relation of parts to the whole. Now joy is evidence of greater expression (or being), sadness witnesses and expresses a loss of involvement with reality.[17]

How is it that Soul can experience sadness if its natural desire is toward unity. The answer involves an understanding of Spinoza's concepts of perfection, adequate cause, and coercion. Perfection and reality are synonymous to unity in totality or substance.[18] Now the parts within the whole can move toward or away from that perfection according to their level of involvement. Perfection for Spinoza means completion in the sense of unity; therefore, no part can be complete but it can be more or less complete.

From this sense of completion there follows the notion of adequate cause. Only substance is *causa sui* but ways of being, including Souls, move toward such a state to the degree that the effects of their being can be clearly perceived to proceed from their participation in unity. "Clearly perceived" and "adequate cause" are therefore also synonymous, since to know through itself and to act through itself is the very meaning of substance. This is the ground of Spinoza's famous dictum that the order of things is the same as the order and connection of ideas.[19]

We can now understand more fully why it is that the "more we know about singular things, the more we know about God."[20] This maxim sums up the relation between perfection and adequate cause. It says that the parts reveal their intelligibility in direct proportion to their proximate participation in unity. Thus, the more reality or perfection Soul enjoys, the more intelligible human life becomes. Conversely, the less reality or perfection Soul enjoys, the more muddled is its involvement with unity. Soul becomes sad because it can forget the whole and concentrate only on the parts. Soul ceases to be the adequately active cause of its relation with unity and becomes a passive witness to its own deterioration. Hence an active emotion is a way of living that moves Soul into union with what is; a passive emotion diminishes Soul's life within the whole. Love, as we shall see, is the paradigm of this harmony of perfection, intelligibility, and adequate cause. However, it should be understood that any passive emotion could become an active one through the transformation brought about by *scientia intuitiva*.

A final word about coercion: it could be said that the entire aim of Spinoza's life was to free Soul from every form of *external coercion*. I say external because Spinoza regards all such uses of force to be futile and misdirected. The reason is that Soul is already *internally* coerced and following out the consequences of this coercion constitutes its goal. To the extent that Soul can follow the traces of this determination back to the sources of unity, to that very same extent Soul is free to be who and what Soul is. A whole that is a genuine unity must be based on internal relations. Externally related wholes are fake unities that disguise their aggregate, nonorganic structure. Soul is free to be human only if it is mindful enough to know intuitively what that means in the practice of daily life. It is its own self-coerced reality that contains the key to its happiness. When Soul acts knowingly through its own being, the internal relations comprising its reality express what it ought to do by reason of who it is. This is *scientia intuitiva* at work.

In the second part of the *Ethics* Spinoza makes distinctions among three ways of knowing.[21] The distinctions among them arise from the degree of unity experienced in their practice. *Imagination*, the first kind, arises from fragmentary and confused sense knowledge and the opinions formed from customary experience. Thus opinion or imaginary ways of knowing result in a pseudopersonal interpretation of a world exhibiting external agency that can be controlled by human power. It is, of course, entirely unreliable and akin to guesswork. The second kind is *ratio* or reason. It arises from adequate knowledge of the properties of things. This type of knowledge brings about shared ideas or *notiones communes* that make up the accepted state of knowledge at a particular time. A good example would be the axioms and definitions of the *Ethics*. Valuable as this is, it is not sufficient for it is inevitably abstract based as it is on universals. This abstractness awaits the healing power of the dynamic, concrete apprehension of the particular as it reflects the unity of the whole. This is *scientia intuitiva*.

Such a way of knowing "advances from an adequate idea of certain attributes of God to the adequate knowledge of the essence of singular things."[22] It has certain specific qualities:

> First, it advances, that is, it admits of degrees of success. In other words it must be practiced. Spinoza practices it in the last part of the *Ethics* where feelings inhabited by this kind of knowing culminate in the *Intellectual Love of God*, Soul's highest human happiness.
> Second, this kind of knowledge is concerned with particulars. It catches events and situations in their concreteness since Soul is mindful of the meanings expressed in the living present.
> Third, It is the felt register of unity.
> Fourth, it is grounded in the Soul's lived experience of internal relations to the whole and is therefore adequate cause of itself in the sense previously discussed.

Let us call Soul that knows this way "mindful soul."[23] The more Soul is mindful of the whole, the more its felt sense of unity expresses joy. Conatus, mindfulness, truth, power, and perfection are all involved in Soul's life. Note that this mindfulness concerns itself with the way in which the idea of God expresses itself in the being of particulars. The human Soul has the power to include in its mindfulness certain atemporal ways of housing the particulars of the world. Soul experiences singular events through the being of God. There is a phrase that expresses this experience, perhaps it even originated with Spinoza's *Ethics*: to see, that is to say, to experience, and express everything *sub specie aeternitatis.* Here "*specie*" means form. Spinoza is quite serious when he calls nature "the face of God." Mindful Soul is mindful of this when it knows God through love. Within this experience unity through involvement replaces the illusion of freedom. We can accept the eternal, necessary order of events and situations. This is akin to the first truth of the Buddha: human life is marked by suffering. Spinoza calls this state "acquiescence." It is neither smug, nor passive, nor indifferent, nor fatalistic. It is best expressed as *Soul satisfaction,* which is "the joy which is produced by being a soul mindful of itself and its own power of acting."[24] True joy is Soul's expression of its intimacy with God or Nature even in the midst of difficulty. Mindful Soul radiates a joy that expresses both acceptance of the way things are and at the same time a determination to express an even greater degree of affirmation of power. The strength of the *Liber* or Free Soul is anchored in its internal relation to that which is one, true, good, and powerful.

Soul is transformed by the third kind of knowledge. What does this mean? In the vast cavernous subjectivity that characterizes being human, there lurks the possibility of a way of life that overcomes the mutilation of reality. When made actual that possibility is called "Love," which Spinoza defines this way: "Love is a joy with the accompanying idea of an external cause."[25] Therefore, love in its ordinary sense is a passive emotion for it makes Soul dependent on another. It is to be understood as leading to human bondage. What is required to transform love from a species of bondage to an active emotion? This is a crucial moment in the *Ethics.* In part 5 Spinoza speaks, as we have seen, of "The Intellectual Love of God" as Soul's highest good and greatest joy. I used "lurks" deliberately as this transformation need not happen and indeed lies at the end of a long and arduous passage.

The passage from a passive emotion to an active one is carried out by *scientia intuitiva.* We see now why Spinoza has taken such pains to define and explain this third kind of knowledge. One should see this journey as a pilgrimage with *scientia intuitiva* as its guide. To express what happens in this transformation from passivity to activity we need to grasp the intellectual love of God as a process and call it Soul's "understanding love toward God," which is part of the infinite love with which God loves himself. At this point subjectivity and objectivity dissolve in the crucible of involvement with an eternal unity. This way of knowing engages the knower and the known in a fusion so intimate that Soul is absorbed into the activity being carried out. Because of this intimacy Soul is able to express what is known by becoming it. This may sound strange, but it occurs almost every day when human beings unify Soul with what is known. For example, one who swims well swims knowingly even though not conscious of swimming. Or there is a person who does a kind act, and then there is someone who character expresses kindness. We say she is a kindly person. Soul is what it knows, and that activity is its knowing.

This act of union expresses directly what Spinoza means by *scientia intuitiva*. When applied to love, however, it takes on a very special significance. Love in this most "perfect" sense is confined solely to God. It expresses Soul's freedom for in this way of being Soul can also experience the eternal, necessary quality of individual expressions. Soul knows them in their unity with God insofar as that is possible for the human Soul. Soul's love expresses through an active power the specific, intricate relations of singular things to reality and thereby celebrates both those things in themselves and its own power of expression in the temporal world. We see also that there are infinite ways of loving since there are infinite ways to be. Soul is called to the finesse of love because each activity demands to be loved in its own way of being. The deftness of Soul's inscape lets the inscape of other expressions express themselves. This also means that Soul can transform a passive emotion into an active emotion any time it can experience that emotion through *scientia intuitiva*. At this point we are reduced to repetition (as the above, "expressions express") since our vocabulary runs thin, and we are forced to call on the poets. It is the fortunate culture that continues to nourish and honor them.

Spinoza's *Ethics* is a song of joy because joy will always conquer sadness. True joy is Soul's expression of its intimacy with God or Nature. Soul in the grip of power radiates a joy that expresses both acceptance of the way things are and at the same time a determination to express an even greater degree of affirmation of power. This is the quality of life enjoyed by the Liber or Free Soul. To understand this power of ideas we must underline Spinoza's understanding of knowing in the third way. An idea is not a mere representation of what is happening. It is itself an affirmation of its content. In fact all of Soul's actions are driven by desire. As already said, this desire Spinoza calls in the Latin, "*conatus*." To the degree that Soul shares in God's understanding, it affirms its own desiring, feeling, thinking, and willing as powerful because true. Spinoza never separates desire from feeling, feeling from thinking, and thinking from willing. Each is together with the other in the spectrum of powers that express the conatus of Soul. This unity of emotions and ideas is the direct outcome of Spinoza's understanding of the relation between body and mind. He maintains that the body is the idea of the mind. And that body and mind are the same thing (conatus) viewed from different perspectives. Soul is a two-sided coin. Viewed from the perspective of the body, Soul is the expression of emotion; viewed from the perspective of mind, Soul is the expression of affirmative ideas. Put another way, body and mind are both abstractions since of themselves they are not substantial enough to contain the fullness of Soul. Since an idea is an affirmation of power and therefore is itself an expression of power, the worst state that Soul can fall into is lack of conviction or incessant wavering as to the truth of an idea. Therefore the key active emotion is *fortitudo* or "strength of mind." It is self-evident that Soul cannot express with appropriate intensity that of which it is not convinced. This intuitive knowledge possesses a concrete connection to the particular presence of certain attributes of God, Nature or Substance. Soul knows things directly in their insistent particularity because Soul experiences the power of God's presence in these particular things. This is knowing in its highest affirmation. To repeat: It is the difference between knowing how to swim and swimming knowingly. Action is the first quality of intuition.

The Liber has reached a level of understanding that permits him to fuse the eternal and the temporal in the formation of his character. This achievement culminates in "the Intellectual Love of God." But before this 'cadence' can occur, the Liber must act in certain defining ways as the world presses in, and emotions thereby rise into existence. Hence Spinoza's detailed analysis of the emotions in parts 2, 3, and 4. There is a convincing and persuasive continuity among all five parts of the *Ethics*. From start to finish we witness the possibility of the rise of Soul's expression of feeling to the very heights of eloquence. Part 1 can be read as proclamation of never-ending creativity as the fundamental character of everything. It is not simply a logical proposition or even an axiom à la geometry. It is a straightforward declaration that reality is expression itself. What confuses readers of the *Ethics* is the drastic shift from cool analytically sophisticated abstractions to the most intimately detailed examination of emotions. Great philosophers are able to do this, but readers are often startled by this conjunction of seeming opposites. But it has always been one of the responsibilities of philosophy to overcome dualisms and set the mind on a wider path than previously imagined. This is precisely what Spinoza achieves in the *Ethics*. He is writing in reaction to Descartes' dualism, which at that time had been the generally accepted theory of reality. His overcoming of this dualism is anchored in logic and a psychology derived from that logic. His initial hypothesis is that wholes are simple, and parts are complex. Parts are compromised in their unity by the fact that they imply and are built upon relations to other parts. That is the very meaning of a part. Spinoza maintains that the plan of the whole determines the functioning of the parts. We can now alter the previous translation of Spinoza's first work from the "Healing of the Mind" to "The Healing of Soul." This recuperation takes place through understanding the proper relation between wholes and parts. Since emotions are confused ideas, the effective philosophical therapy for living a good (that is, ethical) life begins with an examination of the emotions and their power over human behavior. The remedy for the alienated Soul resides first in understanding what is happening and then in attaining the power to express a true, proper, and adequate response to the situations and environments that impose themselves on Soul. I maintain that Soul is a better term than mind because mind is an abstraction and therefore leaves out what ought to be part of the discussion. A careful reading of the *Ethics* would demonstrate that the use of Soul is no threat to brain science. In point of fact part 2, "On the Origin of Mind," as well as the *Ethics* passim constitutes precisely the kind of careful analysis that can accommodate the major tenets of various types of materialism and idealism that have created the jungle out of which I said I needed to escape in order to compose this study. The healing of the Soul requires that we have the right 'take' on things. What causes Soul to lose its way and stumble in its efforts to express reality is a deep and troubled confusion about what is actually happening. Since "Whatever is, is in God, and nothing can be conceived without him,"[26] the solution to all Soul's difficulties lies in this: to create the true attitude toward what is happening and to always grasp reality through God's presence. While not agreeing with Spinoza's metaphysics, Neville comes to a similar conclusion about the need to bring the eternal life of God into Soul's actions and passions.

The reference to 'passions' brings to a close this analysis of Spinoza's way of understanding Soul's emotional life. Since everything that is was or will be is an expression of some kind of power, conflict is an inevitable part of life. Soul is sometimes the actor and sometimes the acted upon, and there is no escape from this situation. The key to the good life is to be found in the identification of Soul's being with power: *To be is to be an expression of power.* Soul has an internal barometer that measures the degree of power it experiences. This is its emotional state. Soul feels either more or less powerful. The degrees of this intensity of feeling range from mere survival to the highest joy conceivable. Parts 3 and 4 of the *Ethics* eloquently express this primordial relation between feeling and expression. It is quite incorrect to think of Spinoza as identifying intellectual experience and emotional experience. He is not saying that Soul can think its way out of emotional states. Spinoza is not that silly. An emotion is a *force*. It has weight, drive, and power. It *affects* Soul, and unless properly understood it can drive Soul into the most dangerous places. What lurks around an emotion is the power to push Soul toward self-destructive behavior. Similarly a true idea is not merely an abstract representation of what is happening in a particular emotional state. Ideas are also powers of expression. They can modify and even replace the negative force that may be affecting Soul. Spinoza closes the *Ethics* with two eloquent passages that may be taken as descriptions of the activities of the Liber:

> [I]n fact he who has a body capable of very considerable activity has a mind which . . . is highly conscious of itself, and of God and of things. In this life, therefore we mainly endeavor that the body of childhood . . . should develop into a body that is capable of a great many activities and is related to a mind that is highly conscious of itself, of God and of things, and in such a way that everything relating to its memory or imagination should be of scarcely any importance in comparison with its intellect.[27]

. . . .

> [T]he wise person scarcely suffers any disturbance of spirit, but being conscious, by virtue, of a certain eternal necessity, of himself, of God and of things, never ceases to be, but always possesses true spiritual contentment.
>
> If the road I have pointed out as leading to this goal seems very difficult, yet it can be found. For if salvation were ready to hand and could be discovered without great toil, how could it be that it is almost universally neglected? All things excellent are as difficult as they are rare.[28]

There is of course much more to the *Ethics* than what this condensed version has presented. In sum Spinoza is telling us that the life of the *Liber* is a meditation on life and never on death.[29] Indeed, the human mind is eternal and therefore we have another connection between Spinoza and the description of eternity and its rewards in Neville.[30] And, finally for those who have struggled with me through this very difficult chapter, I offer part 4, proposition 42: "Laughter (*Hilaritas*) can never be excessive."[31]

6

SOUL WORK

> Call the world if you Please "The vale of Soul-making." . . . Do you not see how necessary a World of Pains and troubles is to school an Intelligence and make it a Soul?
>
> —John Keats, The Letters of John Keats

Given the directions our culture has taken over the last few decades, it will be hard work to recapture the meaning of Soul as both an individual and communal living expression. In previous chapters I underlined the importance of eloquence and poise. They are no less relevant in what follows. In the present chapter I propose to develop in much greater depth and detail the previously discussed ideas of Spinoza as well as more modern updates dealing with the restoration of Soul. I believe that a formidable plan of action can be shaped whereby Soul can succeed in its struggle to express itself. My goal is to offer a reconstruction of Soul so that we human beings can become as far as is possible "masked, practical mystics."[1] In general the steps are as follows:

Practicing some form of meditation daily.
Experiencing the living presence of eternity.
Realizing the potential impact of such an orientation.
Gaining a real feel for alternative actions.
Understanding the relation between body health and mental health.

I begin by returning to Spinoza and the definition of God provided in the sixth definition of part 1 of the *Ethics*. The original Latin reads:

> Per Deum intelligo Ens absolute infinitum, hoc est, substantiam *constantem infinitis attributis*, quorum unumquodque aeternam, & infinitam essentiam exprimit.

> [The traditional definitions do not capture the resonant concreteness of these overwhelmingly powerful words. They fail because they do not express the depths of the words written in bold print. I translate as follows][2]

> By God I understand Being rising up by means of expressing itself in an infinite number of attributes, each of which expresses being eternally and infinitely.[3]

Recall the title of the fourth chapter, "Eloquence Arising." It defined Soul's striving for unified wholeness with God. Here by using the verb *"constare"* to define God, Spinoza stretches the Latin language so as to communicate the self-manifesting power of God. This is very much like the sacred word *YHWH* used in the Old Testament to express the Being of God as "I AM THAT I AM." To rise, to reveal, to manifest, and, finally, *to express* are the fundamental activities of God as experienced by the Jews in the beginning of their history as a people. Though excommunicated, Spinoza never forgot his earliest encounters with an all powerful dimension of existence. Also the echoes of Neoplatonic thought in this understanding of God ought not to be ignored. Finally, the medieval theophanic tradition shares this understanding of the ways in which God remains as continuing cause in the effects. Spinoza would nod in agreement when Plato, Plotinus, and John Scotus Eriugena along with many other thinkers standing in this tradition saw beings (and in fact all creatures) as sparks of divinity. The structure of Spinoza's Divine Power is Expression Itself calling Soul to express its singular activity through its own striving after an adequate "eloquence arising." We now are in possession of a direct connection uniting Soul, eternity, God, Nature, or Substance through the idea of expression.

Keats gives us a clue as to how to use this powerful unity so that Soul can transform itself from abstract intelligence to concretely Soulful activity. The way to heal Soul and let it speak truly and powerfully is through gaining a life that promotes a concrete understanding of human emotions. Spinoza himself tells us that this will require very hard work. The means for such a change in Soul's attitude toward the world is to be found in parts 2, 3, 4, and 5 of the *Ethics*. Human intelligence needs to enter what Keats calls "the World of pains and troubles" and make itself a real Soul. The bloodless and prideful human mind so beloved of philosophers and scientists alike must experience directly the ordeal of human emotions.

Part 4 of the *Ethics* bears the ominous title "Of Human Bondage." We are enslaved by certain of our feelings, and if left untreated, they prevent the rise of human eloquence. In fact they stifle expression itself. They are Soul killers, but Spinoza points out a way to loosen their grip and restore to Soul a sense of freedom. Spinoza's theory of the emotions involves recognizing that our emotions cause a change in the pitch of our consciousness. This alteration in our moods can be understood as either increasing or decreasing our connection with reality. Spinoza's metaphysics provides a normative measure for assessing the healthiness of our emotional life. What is at stake is the intensity of our sense of self-affirmation, and this in turn is proportionate to the degree of reality that our Soul is able to express. Since reality is the continuous outcome of God's power to express, it is obvious that attaining adequate truth should be the major part of Soul therapy. The more truth Soul possesses, the more powerful it is, or said in a different way, the more intimate Soul's connection with the really real, the greater Soul's power to express itself. The road to adequate truth and therefore real power lies in Soul's grasp of Spinoza's three kinds of knowledge: imagination, reason, and *scientia intuitiva*. The previous chapter dealt with this subject matter in a less than organized way. Emotions are confused ideas and the result of ignorance concerning their true meaning. This confusion can be caused by many factors, but the paramount culprits are cultural biases, knowledge gained only through the senses, knowledge gained through random experience, and the false signs that proliferate in our culture. Those gripped by such feelings truly live in a world of delusion. Spinoza's says, "I shall henceforth call such knowledge of the first kind, opinion or imagination."[4]

Reason, the second form of knowledge, may also be called "science." This type of knowing surveys the true and necessary character of things and their relations and is called the use of "Common Notions" and "adequate ideas of the properties of things"[5] by which Spinoza means those laws, discoveries, composition of relations, and in general what the true science of the day has so far understood to be the nature of things. In this kind of knowledge relief from bondage can be had because these ideas are adequate enough to let Soul see the external causes of things and results in "common notions" that can help move Soul out of some emotional states in which it may be mired. But it is ultimately ineffective because this kind of knowledge is too general and abstract. Freud once told someone that seeking psychoanalytic treatment through learning about the principles and theories of psychoanalysis was the equivalent of handing a starving person a menu. No real nourishment can be found in this way of knowing. When they are experienced, emotions are always personal and individual. Each Soul can gain from these common notions (e.g., the definitions and axioms of the *Ethics*), but Soul's emotions are uniquely its own and must be treated as such. This can only occur in Keats's school of "pain and troubles." Soul needs the third form of knowing, *scientia intuitiva*, for true and lasting self-transformation. *Scientia intuitiva* both respects the individuality of Soul's emotional responses and at the same time connects them in the most intimate manner with the essence of Substance, God, or Nature.

The basis of Spinoza's theory of the emotions lies in his doctrine of *conatus,* by which he means the evident fact that Soul and everything else in the universe seeks to express and thereby preserve its own being. This flows from the idea of Substance, God, or Nature as a self-causing infinite power of self-expression. Desire is the best way to understand *conatus* as the primordial dimension of Soul's existence. All things in the universe therefore share in this desire to live expressively and endure. God is the "indwelling and not the transient cause,"[6] and Soul along with other existing beings feels this power as it asserts its right to be here.

There are two kinds of emotions. There are feelings that cause Soul to be passive because they are generated by external forces. However, active emotions affirm and enhance the power of Soul's being because they are grounded in a true grasp of Soul's relation to its situation. Inadequate knowledge involves vagueness, confusion, and weakness. Adequate knowledge involves clarity, precision, and power. Hence truth that results from adequate knowledge (knowledge of the second kind [*ratio*-science]) but most especially knowledge of the third kind, *scientia intuitiva* renders Soul powerful and to the extent possible in control. Truth for Spinoza is always graded in terms of its adequacy for understanding states of affairs.

Spinoza's algorithm for living a happy life is clear. The more adequate knowledge Soul possesses, the more intimate is its connection with reality; the stronger that connection, the more powerful is Soul; and the more Soul experiences active feelings, the more its *conatus* strives to express itself. With this formula in hand let us look at certain emotions and how they affect Soul's power to express. Parts 3 and 4 contain lengthy inventories of emotions and how they affect Soul and what causes them.

There are three primary emotions from which all others flow by way of contrast or complexity. We have already seen the first, *conatus*, which is the drive to maintain, sustain, and grow one's being. Coupled to this base line of feeling are the other two emotions—Joy and Sorrow. Joy expresses the feeling of enhanced power, whereas sadness expresses diminished power.[7] Joy grants Soul pleasure, while sadness gives it pain. From this unitary triad there follows derivative complex emotions expressed and explained in propositions 33–59. Then Spinoza gathers these emotions into a set of "Definitions of Emotion" (there are forty-eight of them) and then concludes part 3 with a "General Definition of the Emotions." The causes and therapies of these emotions are treated in part 4, which concludes with an appendix in which Spinoza collects under main headings what he has said "about the right way of living."[8] These parts of the *Ethics* open a powerful path toward making possible Soul's "Eloquence Arising."

Human happiness is governed by its achieved degree of unity with Substance, God, or Nature. Like barometers, our emotions tell us how close or distant is our relation with God, Nature or Substance. A brief discussion of the ways in which the three primary emotions as well as some of the complex derivative emotions function to enhance or diminish Soul's union with God or Nature or Substance will help us grasp the level of eloquence arising achieved by Soul. When joy or sorrow is the expression of our relation to "All-There-Is,"[9] there is evidence that adequate or inadequate truth is at work in Soul's *conatus*. I will now select certain other emotions which bear upon our contemporary culture. The single most important derivative emotion is "self-esteem": "Self-esteem is really the highest thing we can hope for. For no one strives to preserve his being for the sake of any end (as we have shown in IV P 25), and because this self-esteem is more and more encouraged and strengthened by praise (by III P 53 C), and on the other hand more and more upset by blame (by III, P. 55 C), we are guided most by love of esteem and can hardly bear a life in disgrace."[10] Legitimate self-esteem powers Soul to an active life. Two emotions often confused with self-esteem are pride and humility. Both bring Soul down in different ways: pride leads Soul to think "more highly of itself than is just"[11] while "sadness" arises from too harsh a judgment on Soul's powers of existence.[12] Love is a complex emotion. On the one hand, it can lessen our power because it can be caused by an external object. The verb "to swoon" says it all. On the other hand, the "Intellectual Love of God" is our highest blessedness. Therefore there is a type of love that is connected to an internal cause. The conclusion of the *Ethics* will show this thoughtful emotion and/or emotional thought to be the source of Spinoza's idea of human blessedness.

Before coming to that supreme moment, it remains to define some of the emotions that are characteristic of our time and that lessen Soul's power.[13] *Hatred* is pain, accompanied by the idea of an external cause (def. 7). *Anger* is the desire by which through hatred we are induced to injure someone whom we hate (36). *Envy* is hatred, insofar as it induces a man to be pained by another's good fortune or to rejoice in another's evil fortune (def. 23). *Ambition* is the immoderate desire of power (def. 42). *Greed* is the excessive desire and love of riches (def. 47). *Honor* ("*Gloria*") is pleasure accompanied by the idea of some action of our own, which we believe to be praised by others (def. 30).[14] *Derision* is pleasure arising from our conceiving the presence of a quality, which we despise, in an object which we hate (def. 11). Our age thrives on these negative feelings, but they lead directly to a diminishment, if not the very disappearance, of Soul as an expressive power to be. Given these emotions that set the circumstances of our bondage (and there are others that could be mentioned), the question of human liberation looms large. Is there a way out of servitude to our passive emotions?

A passive emotion can be transformed into an active one through the following steps. First, an emotion is a confused idea. It is therefore the most inadequate form of knowing and arises from our body's contact with external objects. Second, we are often unaware of the bodily base of our emotional life. Our jaws clench, our muscles tense, adrenalin builds up, and so on and so forth. Therefore, the third step in the transformation of passive emotions to active ones is to become aware of our bodily states. We are usually unaware of these bodily reactions because we do not wish to acknowledge such emotions. Denial will not help. Self-acceptance is the fourth step required to transform destructive feeling. How can one deal with a problem unless one acknowledges that one has it? Assuming the above four steps have occurred, then recalling that the mind even in its confused state is still the idea of the body, understanding can begin to seek the causes of our disturbance. Even here a preliminary step is needed because often it is our beliefs about the causes of our distress that are at the heart of our distress. Our beliefs can easily distort or misinterpret the causes bringing about our passivity. Supposing, then, that all these steps have been successfully carried out, at that moment the fact of the world being a totally determined structure may come to the fore, and we can take inside our minds and bodies what is really going on. Transformation is achieved when we can experience these feelings as the inevitable results of factors reaching backwards in time perhaps even beyond our understanding. But adequate ideas are affirmative powers. Such ideas can move to the third kind of knowledge, *scientia intuitiva*, where their power of intuitive knowing can take up singular events, situations, and persons and lessen or even defuse passive emotions. Once this occurs, then our journey toward becoming Free Persons (Liber) can once again resume.

The last propositions of part 4 of the *Ethics* introduce Spinoza's concrete portrayal of the Free Person (or Liber).[15] The description is compelling. The Free Person's wisdom is a meditation on life, and he scarcely ever thinks about death. The power of the Free Person is expressed as much in avoiding dangers as in overcoming them. The Free Person strives as much as possible to avoid the favors of the ignorant. Only Free Persons are genuinely grateful to each other. A Free Person always acts honestly and shuns deception. A Free Person, guided by reason, is freer in a state where she lives in common decisions than in solitude where she obeys only herself. Spinoza ends this description of the Liber by pointing out the strength of character *(fortitudo)* needed to enable the Liber to live in this manner. This strength is composed of two powers, civility (in the Latin, *generositas*[16]) and strength of mind (in Latin, *animositas* which means "filled with expressive Soul"). I believe that the phrase *strength of mind* concretely sums ups what we must develop and put to work if the contemporary version of the bondage of the emotions is to be broken.

At the end of the fourth part of the *Ethics*, Spinoza provides a richly detailed appendix on "the right way to live." It is required reading for all who would seek to follow Spinoza's way. This is not the place to examine each of his 32 guidelines, but his concluding words do bear repeating for he states unequivocally that such is the power of this way of thinking and acting that even hatred can be transformed into love. We are told, "Hatred can never be good," and "Laughter (*Hilaritas*) can never be excessive." Also: "He who wishes to avenge wrongs by hating in return surely lives miserably. On the other hand, he who is eager to overcome Hate by Love strives joyously and confidently, resists many men as easily as one, and requires the least help from fortune. Those whom he conquers yield joyously, not from a lack of strength but from an increase in their powers. All these things follow so clearly and simply from the definitions of Love and of intellect, that there is no need to demonstrate them separately."[17]

Liber is a synonym for the healthy Soul. To be free is to express one's self with the least internal and external constraint possible. When this becomes a pattern of human conduct, then honor (*"Gloria"*) is the healthy society's response to such an achievement.[18] Spinoza opens the last part of the *Ethics* with these words, "I pass, finally, to the remaining Part of the *Ethics*, which presents the means or way, leading to Freedom."

Some contend that this part is too mystical to be worthy of the logical power of Spinoza's work. Others see in it a way to grow new eyes so that the world, our place in it, and God's relation to us can be felt in an entirely different light. I side with the latter. First, its brevity is the result of the logical power accumulating throughout the first four parts. Second, it brings together three themes that run through the *Ethics* and express the full intent of Spinoza's endeavor to express Soul's meaning at the very beginning of the modern age. They are *Unity, Wholeness,* and *Integrity*. Understanding their central place in the endeavor of Soul work helps to open up the "mystical portion" of the *Ethics*. Unity is the essential message of Spinoza's *Ethics*, and it comes to final fruition in the fifth part. Unity is felt most intensely as *the Intellectual Love of God* as constituting the highest happiness attainable by Soul. "Intellectual" is too abstract to capture the meaning of Spinoza's ultimate transformation of Soul. "Spiritual" is Neal Grossman's apt suggestion for a substitute term closer to Spinoza's meaning and more in tune with our current cultural situation.[19] The attainment of this experience is the result of *scientia intuitiva's* power to conceive things under the aspect (*species*) of eternity.[20] This spiritual experience is progressive and moves through specific stages and has certain characteristics. It is concrete and not abstract for it deals with particular beings. It is continuous and not intermittent. Thereby satisfying Spinoza's desire for a good that is continuous as expressed in his first work, the *de Emendatione Intellectus*,[21] or as previously translated "The Healing of the Mind." It is reflexive moving toward the interiority of the person and not outward toward the world of objects. Therefore, it is the union of the mind with the whole of nature; it is a joy which ever feeds itself upon the sources of its own dynamic; it is sure of its own true authenticity; and its home is the nature of God.[22]

Part 5 of the *Ethics* can be divided into three sections.

> The identification of the source of human freedom. What the *Liber* experiences is the power of clear and distinct conceptions of the passive emotions which render them part of the mind and, hence, subject to human persons rather than part of their bondage. (Propositions 1–13)

The discovery of the Authentic Source of Human Blessedness. This the intellectual love of god. This Love consists of the proper referral of all things to their genuine source—God or Nature. (Propositions 14–22)

The ideal life as Conscious Union with God. (Propositions 21–42)

Involved in this last achievement are the following: the meaning of eternity, the eternity of the human mind, and the gradations of eternal thought. Spinoza's concept of eternity is not to be confused with mere duration; rather eternity is the expression of the timelessly necessary existence of God's essence. This eternity is not 'immortality,' life after death, or indefinite existence.[23] The eternity of the human mind is experienced to the degree that it shares through adequate ideas the life of the divine mind, and therefore to that same degree, the human mind is already eternal. That there are gradations of eternal thought is grounded in the principle that a mind is more real; that is, the more eternal, the more there is of it. Now due to the method of reflexive thought, the more adequate ideas a being has, the more it exists as fully real (the *conatus*). Therefore, the more active our mind is with adequate ideas, the more we are ourselves; hence, the more we are truly ourselves, that is to say, the more we are an expression of God.

Reason (or *ratio*) while necessary to give us the right perspective on nature, does not bear with it the required self-reflexive character since it concerns the true order of cause and effect. *Scientia intuitiva*, on the other hand, is precisely that self-conscious type of knowledge, which, if pushed to its ideal limit, renders a human being conscious of union with All-There-Is. Thus the Liber (the Free Person) becomes concretely conscious of the fact that she is a mode or expression of divine existence.

At this peak of spiritual experience the emotional side of the human person is fused with the *Intellectual Love of God* whereby the human person loves God as himself, which is in effect the very love with which God loves Himself. For Spinoza the singular is involved with everything else, and the particular is thereby granted its own standing in the universe. This is what the phrase *sub specie aeternitatis* actually means for that which is conceived through its formal essence must be experienced as an expression of God's being. Within this utterly interior relation with God in thought, it is impossible to act toward a thing without acting toward God. *Conatus* has reached its final point of striving. Wholeness and integrity along with unity have been attained.

What constitutes human blessedness (or happiness) is the fact that in the most complete thinking of which we are capable, our thought is God's thought; and God's thought is God thinking insofar as he constitutes the essence of our mind. All this is to say that God's thought is *our* thinking. This experienced unity of our intelligent being with God merges us with the divine thought. By that very fact, this divine thought more fully characterizes us and gives us our "self." In this spiritual experience the transfusion of our thinking being by God's being renders us more real with the divine reality. God is real in and as us: Once again we can say: Unity and Wholeness joined to Integrity has been attained.

With the closing of this exposition of Spinoza's *Ethics*, we can return to the goals announced at its beginning. Our subject matter is "Soul Work." Perhaps we can now experience more concretely the words with which Spinoza concludes his *Ethics*: "All things excellent are as difficult as they are rare."[24] To sum up: in his own unique manner Spinoza has stressed the importance of *unity, wholeness, and integrity*. Are there contemporary practices that can generate the full eloquence of the human Soul? I suggest that some—if not all—of the following activities can lead human beings forward on the path to fulfillment:

> Practicing some form of meditation daily. This practice regularly provides direct access to the concrete experience of unity.
> Experiencing the living presence of eternity. From a Spinozistic point of view meditating on a daily basis brings us an intimate experience of the fact that our mind is part of a 'higher mind,' God's Mind if you will.[25] Furthermore if we take the history of human experience seriously we understand that human beings in many different forms of spiritual meditation have had similar experiences. The Buddha says in these matters, one must trust his or her experience. So here we also meet Hegel's search for *die Sache Selbs't* which we may identify as a supreme moment of integration between the subjective and the objective dimensions of human experience. Aristotle and Plotinus speak of the mystical experience of *'nous nousing.'* Then there is Plato's *Seventh Letter* and its flame that suddenly bursts forth when philosopher and student think together. And to bring matters up to the present there is Robert Pirsig's pursuit of 'Quality' throughout his masterful *Zen and the Art of Motorcycle Maintenance*. And we ought

not to forget the stunning description of the mystical experience shared by Monica and Augustine in the IX Book of the Confessions: "WHAT IS; I AM WHO AM/ YAHWEH."[26] One must grasp the structural integrity of such moments. For Spinoza what happens in these moments is that we know particular things in the way God does. This is exactly what knowing all-there-is through the formal (divine) aspects of particulars actually means. This act is grounded in the experience of the wholeness of all-there-is—within time and of no time. Meditation concretely demonstrates what Spinoza speculatively put forth as the theological consequence of his metaphysical system. There is some part of our minds that is eternal because we can know and also experience the necessarily eternal ideas and emotions of God because we are at the level brought on by mediation (*scientia intuitiva*). The emotional and felt experience of the thoughts of God's mind are one and same. Thus we can participate and share in those qualities of the infinite Ideas of God and the infinite kinds of affects. This experience is direct, conscious, and full of *conatus* or joyful energy. What was said briefly in the previous chapter can now be more fully understood. One might read every book about swimming and consider himself knowledgeable about swimming. But that is not even close to what Spinoza means by the INTELLECTUAL LOVE OF GOD. It is (as said before and remains but a feeble example) the difference between knowing about swimming and swimming knowingly. This is the active knowing that unites, makes whole, and integrates human life in its struggle to merge the eternal and the temporal. The impact of such an orientation whereby the eternal and temporal come together turns the world upside down and reverses what is important.

Gaining a real feel for alternative actions. Previously I argued for the importance of seeing consciousness as a form of contrast. There could be no greater contrast than that of the temporal and the eternal. Its supreme gift is to provide humans with a genuine sense of proportion between what is, what was, and what can be. In the most important moments of our life we exist on the knife edge of decision. What follows from the contrast between the temporal and the eternal is an intense awareness of what is at stake in our most important moments. A real feel for alternatives at this level of the plane of human existence is the opportunity to make wise choices that move us beyond mere personal advantage. This enlargement of our vision is critical for human growth and development. Both personal and social value hinge on understanding what is really at stake in the ultimate choices we make. I say *feel* deliberately for this is not a simple intellectual exercise. Felt intelligence is what brings us clarity and motivation, which are the most important strengths we need to bring to critical human moments. That is why Spinoza speaks directly and concretely of human bondage and human freedom. Gaining a real feel for the ultimate dimensions of our experience banishes any flippant attitude toward our place in the cosmos. The Buddha says that there are three poisons that kill the Soul, sometimes quickly and sometimes slowly—*greed, hatred, and delusion*. Are these not at the root of our contemporary crisis? Experiencing the contrast between the temporal and the eternal can move us beyond mere personal advantage, envy of others, and the insanity that stalks our lives.

Understanding the relation between bodily health and mental health. These practices provide us an opportunity to bring knowledge and action together. As Wang Yang-ming said: "One who is supposed to know, and does not act, does not know."[27] They also underscore, stress, and give concrete evidence of the unity, wholeness, and integrity that are the ultimately important factors in Soul work. What stands in the way of seeing Spinoza's insistence upon the importance of meditation for Soul work that leads to a healing of the mind is confusion over what he means by psychophysical parallelism. I agree with Donald Davidson's judgment that "the mental and the physical are just two ways of viewing and understanding one and the same world.[28] This separation of mind and body is very difficult for moderns to swallow, and it is made even more indigestible by Spinoza's insistence that the mind can affect the body even as the body can affect the mind. Such causal interaction between a spiritual and physical reality seems impossible to contemporary scientists and neuro-philosophers. Given science's absolute theoretical separation between the mental and the physical, it appears that Spinoza has made a blunder of the most egregious kind. Gilbert Ryle might have called it a colossal "category mistake." But such judgments ignore Spinoza's firm adherence to the 'identity' theory of causality: what happens in the body happens in the mind and what happens in the mind happens in the body. But the connection is neither physical nor spiritual. Rather it is the result of the identity of these two abstractions (body and mind). The human person is a whole no matter how science may wish to separate it into parts. Marx Wartofsky explains this in a most lucid manner:

> The radical rejection of this view is a rejection both of a mechanistic determinism of psychic states by bodily states . . . and of a psychic determination of bodily states. For if one takes the identity theory seriously . . . every change in a psychic state is a change in a bodily state, necessarily; but not causally. A change in the psychic character, or intensity, or quality of an emotion does not *lead* to a change in a bodily state; it *is* one. Thus, the mistaken notion that Spinoza proposes a parallelism similar to interactionism as against a Cartesian interactionism has the model wrong. There is a conceptual parallelism, insofar as we think of bodies and minds. But what we think, under these two attributes, is not parallel but identical.[29]

Now for my purposes this way of understanding the relation between the body and the mind contains within itself the ground of my suggested ways to live in this "Vale of Soul Making" without vacillation of mind or weakness of character or pessimism or nihilism. Our *conatus* or drive toward life can move toward joy even in the most difficult circumstances. Joy will always conquer sadness because it has greater strength than sadness. Identity means that from the viewpoint of the whole there is no separation between mind and body. However, from the viewpoint of the parts, there is great complexity as to how these parts can interact. Remember from the viewpoint of Spinoza's metaphysics wholes are simple, and parts are complex. There is only one substance that is simplicity itself, and there are an infinite number of attributes and their accompanying modes. Parts, like body and mind, are therefore complex because they are relations that require other relations for their full expression. Thus does Spinoza completely reverse the commonly held assumption that parts are simple and wholes complex. Also and most important, concepts like 'body' and 'mind' are, as was said before, prime examples of the 'fallacy of misplaced concreteness.' The error in employing such conceptual terms lies in their extreme abstractness. Every abstraction by its very definition leaves something out—in this case, the relation between body and mind. There never was a human being that was just a body, and there never was a human being that was just a mind. But there are and were and will be human beings who are both mindful and embodied. Abstraction makes forms of wholeness impossible for human persons. It does the same for the expressive power of the human Soul. Wholeness is one side of Spinoza's therapy for the healing of the mind and the body. Its achievement moves along these lines of force. Wholeness has no parts. It is often a temptation to confuse wholeness with forms of aggregates. Wholeness is not to be confused with aggregates. In point of fact viewing the human being as an aggregate of parts is precisely what causes the confused ideas that are the equivalent of Spinoza's definition of negative emotions. When wholeness is spoken about on the plane of the human Soul, what is being expressed is an exemplary coherence of parts such that the parts fuse together in forms of coherence that reinforce themselves so that they fully integrate with each other. There is 'no other to this other' since particularity trumps empty wholeness just as Hegel called out Schelling on "that night on which all cows are black." Last, this wholeness on the human plane never achieves completeness because time eats away the integuments bonding it together. In a process world, whether it be Spinoza's unique self-creating (*causa sui*) substance or Whitehead's "perpetually perishing" occasions of experience, time erodes completion because there is no thing such as perfection. Using these insights let us take a more practical look at the list of previously recommended activities leading to an identification of Soul's full expression.

Width and depth enlarge our options, which are no longer locked up in our personalities. Our ego is free to look for alternatives that fit better with what is going on. Choice, intelligence, and wisdom come together to inform our newly integrated selves with a strength of mind no longer chained down by deluded egotistical points of view. What is most significant in this process of widening a human viewpoint is feeling the power of contrast as the real presence of an alternative. Instead of being bogged in the stalemate of fixed points of view, the human mind can begin to see ways out. Now a contrast is *not* a comparison. Rather it is a wider point of view that ideally incorporates opposed points of view. Artists regularly do this, and when they are successful, we feel the inferiority of previous modes of expression. We feel it intensely and do not just intellectually agree. This is the gift of realizing in our Soul the feeling of a new orientation brought on through the practices suggested.

Unity through meditation brings to human experience what materialism leaves out. By denying the existence of Soul, contemporary science is left with no way to provide for the unity that is so central to human existence. Consider the insistence on bodily posture that most meditative traditions insist upon. Consider the act of mental concentration that the various traditions regard as the center of their practice. Consider what happens here: the concrete expression of the unity of the mind and body in action. Human beings are distinguished by the harmony that brings together the abstractions of body and mind. This mingling of different aspects of human beings has its degrees of success and failure. When we speak of the superb athlete, it is the aspect of the body that is stressed; conversely, when we speak of the genius it is the aspect of the mind that is emphasized. The Daoist master Chuang Tzu-tse speaks approvingly of the following words of Confucius:

> The goal of fasting [of the heart] is inner unity. This means hearing but not with the ear; hearing, but not with the understanding; hearing with the spirit, with your whole being. . . . But the hearing of the spirit is not limited to any one faculty, to the ear, or to the mind. Hence it demands the emptiness of all the faculties. And when the faculties are empty, the whole being listens. There is then a direct grasp of what is right there before you that can never be heard with the ear or understood with the mind. Fasting of the heart empties the faculties, frees you from limitation and from preoccupation. Fasting of the heart begets unity and freedom.[30]

Now when you can get a Daoist master to agree with Confucius, you are really onto something! What meditation brings to the human Soul is "a direct grasp" of reality. By granting unity, meditation brings us into the full presence of the real. That is why Soul is expression itself. Soul work demands emptying Soul so that it catches what is real and expresses it. Most often that expression is silence, which to my mind is a perfectly apt expression of what has been understood by Soul.

Wholeness is the result of understanding the difference between the eternal and the temporal. Human experience is enriched by feeling the contrast between the temporal and the eternal. This is a rare occurrence—one not often granted to human beings. But once had, it widens and deepens Soul's sense of reality. It lets Soul understand that besides things that are in time, there are also things that are not in time. Some sense of divinity is certainly involved, but expressing it is an entirely different matter. We look to the artists to help us with this kind of experience, or sometimes silence is enough. What I mostly want to emphasize here is the way in which the possible enters temporal experience and thereby sheds its timelessness through its actualization. Possibilities are eternal; otherwise, they would not be possible. They would be actual. So here is another conundrum that arises when we speak of the eternal. The previous chapter has already dealt at length with the contrast between the possible and the actual. Contrasts are first of all felt and only later understood. They are "flashes of insight"[31] and arise from long and deep meditative thinking. What these flashes do is widen Soul's horizons and declare that the present is not all that we have.

Once unity and wholeness are experienced through felt intelligence, then *integrity* becomes a real possibility. This is not to say it is an automatic result of the previous qualities of conscientiousness. Human beings must "work" at it. Keats is on the mark. We do need pain and suffering if we are to have a real Soul and not, as Hegel would put it, just a "Beautiful Soul."[32] As we saw, Spinoza tells in the final pages of the ethics that our duty is to grow from being a baby to that of full adulthood. It is very hard work. I have already quoted the famous final words of the *Ethics*. Perhaps they bear repeating: "If the way we have pointed seems hard, why should it not be so. For if salvation lay ready to hand, why are there not more happy people. But we must always remember that all things excellent are as difficult as they are rare."[33] The image of the baby is helpful here. Babies cry. Adults speak. Soul is expression.

7

SIGNS OF THE TIMES

> It perhaps once been a hunting dog, perhaps left for dead in the mountains or by some highwayside. Repository of ten thousand indignities. The dog raised its misshapen head and howled weirdly. . . . [T]he dog howled again and began to run, hobbling brokenly on its twisted legs with the strange head agoggle on its neck. As it went it raised its mouth sideways and howled again with a terrible sound. Something not of this earth. As if some awful composite of grief had broke through from the preterite world. It tottered away up the road in the rain on its stricken legs and as it went it howled again and again in its heart's despair until it was gone from all sight and all sound in the night's onset.
>
> —Cormac McCarthy, *The Crossing*

In the *Sophist*, Plato speaks of " 'the Great Battle of the Giants,'" which for him was the struggle to name what is really real—Being that dwelt in lifeless, frozen permanence or Becoming that is always changing and therefore never really is.[1] We, too, dwell in the midst of a great war. I call it the "struggle for our attention." It is easy to round up the usual suspects: market capitalism, consumerism, materialism, and the breakdown of our institutions. It is also necessary to add the fallout from the Bush years: the disrespect for law, the decision to promote and carry out forms of torture, the attack on the Constitution, the failure of the universities to speak out against this rape of our values, and finally the cooperation of the media with this unprecedented and vile assault on our values. In the midst of this terrible scene (now made worse by the breakdown of the global financial order) I still maintain that Soul remains the eloquent amphibian that expresses the two regions of human experience: the eternal and the temporal.

It is important to place these signs of the times within the framework of this effort to reconstruct Soul as expression. We human beings name everything that comes into our environment. We name our children, our pets, our plants, our houses, our streets, our neighborhoods, and even our lovers with special and often secret names. In our time a darker side to this obsession with naming has emerged. We seek to "brand" certain things. This human trait was once confined first to the world of the animals marking out their territories, and then it moved to the world of ranchers and cowboys. Present times have seen it become the realm of advertising and consumption. Recently, it has reached out even to institutions of higher learning. A university president in a cash-strapped institution hires a professional "branding agency" in order to make his university distinctive and recognizable. This is the height of deception. Universities should be distinguished by their faculty and their graduates, not by logos, markers, or other forms of identity recognition.

These signs of the times demand a deeper analysis than that provided by economics, consumer psychology, or the phrase *Everybody does it*. In the midst of this confusion, it is very instructive to once again turn to the philosophy of Charles Sanders Peirce (1839–1914), the great American philosopher who created a stunning expressive metaphysics. To recall, he hypothesized that everything in the world was a sign and that its metaphysical reality resided in the sign structures that expressed the meaning of these beings. Peirce suggested that there were three levels of signs—firstness, secondness, and thirdness. Thoughtful persons interested in inquiring deeply into their culture had to learn to count to three. Each mode of expression had its special function and cultural effects. Firstness expressed itself in icons. These iconic idioms were (as the Greek origin of the word suggests) likenesses of the reality under consideration. Icons were marked by the qualities of freshness and novelty. They were, as Peirce said, attempts to express the world as it was on the first day of creation. As such an icon has exceptional powers of engagement. It is striking in its newness. It expresses what was never heard, seen, or thought before. But icons have a certain shallowness and instability for they remain untested in the world of actual experience. Secondness tests firstness by requiring icons to reveal more fully the depths of their reality. Secondness expresses itself as an index. It points toward the consequences and qualitatively richer aspects of icons. An index is confrontational. It asks an icon to prove itself in the actual world of hard won experience. So, for example, the expression

Where there is smoke, there is fire demands that the iconic novelty of smoke show itself as having certain real consequences. If it cannot pass the tests of secondness, its power as a cultural sign fades and eventually is replaced by a replica or is changed into a more stable and effective sign. Our culture is besotted with icons. Drunk with a fake power of engagement we require more and more of these likenesses of the real. For every Madonna there is a "new Madonna" in the making. For every Michael Jordan, there is "another Michael" in the making. And so it goes. Insofar as our cultural signs remain at the level of firstness, we must move from novelty to novelty in order to remain conscious. An inevitable thinness that is mired in fantasy is the sign of the triumph of firstness. How else do we explain the proliferation of "sequels" in the film world? Spinoza's words cited at the end of the preceding chapter bear repeating, for the world of firstness is really at its deepest level the world of the infant. What is desired above all else is engagement. As soon as we become bored, we are offered a replacement, which is usually just more of the same dressed up in new clothes. Gimmicks dominate. The word *exciting* becomes the highest praise that can be bestowed on any aspect of culture. I also maintain that much of what passes for postmodern "deconstructive" philosophy is simply the shuffling of icons that dazzle but do not teach.

But suppose secondness does its job and expresses compelling indices of what will happen if certain unworthy icons come to dominate the expressions of Soul? Then a process of growth in meaning becomes possible. How does this happen. Well, as we all know one + two = three! A sign has passed through the tough challenges of secondness and has become a symbol. But symbol here does not mean some solitary achievement enjoyed only by a privileged few. Symbols must be taken up by whole communities if their meaning as a sign of the times is to be expressed. Thirdness hails the arrival of unified agreement on the significance of a symbol. Consider the following example. A wedding ring is purchased. Excitement abounds as the icon of a new relation of love is expressed. As an icon, the wedding ring arouses the community to the possibilities of love. Then the wedding ring passes through the mountains, gorges, and valleys of married life. Secondness tests the strength and creativity of the spouses. It is only after significant indexical moments of fidelity, trust, and sacrifices that the community recognizes the enduring power of love. One more symbol of love expresses to the community (that is also always being tested) that a life lived through joy and sorrow, courage and fear (and by extension all the other emotions analyzed by Spinoza) has expressed itself to its members. The wedding ring has attained the status of a symbol.

Symbols require interpretations. By themselves they are merely dead chunks of matter. But a symbol is humankind's most precious achievement for it expresses a fusion of the emotional and the intelligible. Furthermore, to truly understand a symbol, one must participate in it. Symbolic life is not the same as going to the movies. It is real. It is demanding. It enjoins on us the obligation to enter into its meaning. Symbolic life has hidden depths that are only revealed to those who live it concretely. Thus the circle closes on Peirce's doctrine of signs. The meaning of any symbol is wrapped up in the destiny of the community. Interpretation is a precondition for expressing the full speech of a symbol.

Therefore interpretation is the life of the community when it is expressed as the full commitment of the community. But interpretation is just that: a construal of the meaning of the symbolic expression of the community. It is destined to change just as it is destined to provoke disagreement ranging from the trivial to the most serious. In fact, when disagreement reaches the level of absolute disagreement, then the community has perished.

Aristotle maintained that Soul was the origin and sign of life. In many ways that definition remains the most powerful expression of Soul understood as expression. A living community is committed to the development and growth of the meaning of its symbolic expression. It may take a long time for a community to die; even now there are communities seemingly still alive but in fact quite dead to the *meaning* of their symbols. I believe that our present culture is at a perilous point in time. It hovers between life and death. Its destiny cannot be foretold, but two great signs struggle over Soul's power to express itself fully.

One Sign Is DIVERSION: The Other Is MINDFULNESS

By diversion I mean the actual way our culture incessantly and deliberately distracts Soul's mindfulness. It does so by establishing a series of concentric circles that trap Soul and deepen its fall into an inevitable speechlessness. The origin of the word *infant* is the Latin *infans*, which literally means "the speechless one." The goal of the culture of diversion is to weaken and finally eliminate Soul's power to express itself. By reducing Soul to dumbness, it aims to silence Soul. Our culture is determined to carry out a culture of diversion whereby any authentic difference is not allowed to express itself. Once it succeeds in this undertaking, humankind becomes an easily manipulated herd, and from that point onward culture is free to create distortions, delusions, and unnecessary needs. Mark this phrase: "unnecessary needs." It is itself a contradiction for if a need is unnecessary, then it is not a need. And yet the circular currents that produce the sign of diversion incessantly proclaim the existence and, more importantly, the availability of these unnecessary needs. In what follows I shall try to describe some of the circles that, serpentlike, entwine Soul in a spiral of false desires. Inevitably, Soul's *conatus* is enfeebled, and a shallow flatness spreads itself over the community of consumers and its devotees.

I offer an image of the contemporary Soul. It is that of Laocoon as described by Vergil in his *Aeneid* and as expressed in the well-known tortuous Hellenistic sculpture. Laocoon had warned the Trojans not to accept the gift horse presumably left in tribute by the seemingly defeated Greeks. Vergil gives him the immortal words, "I fear the Greeks but most especially the Greeks bearing gifts."[2] A priest of Neptune and a strong but aging warrior, he is punished by the gods for expressing this warning. It will be the last words he will ever express. Two horribly large serpents emerge from the sea and coil themselves around him and his two young sons and devour all of them. The fact that youth is here joined to maturity adds to the poignancy of the battle for Soul's attention. I ask that you bear Laocoon in mind as we survey these serpents that spiral upwards in ever tightening coils as they seek to divert Soul from its source of creative mindfulness.

The coil of the first serpent of diversion rises to the surface by reason of our capitalist market-driven culture. If it is to survive, a market-driven reality must capture the attention of consumers. If they are to buy, consumers must be engaged by the imaginative expressions created by advertisers. It is the law of the market that more and more "goods" must be produced and consumed if its values are to survive. Without continuous but very questionable "growth," the market falters, and capitalism enters upon a death spiral. It is therefore absolutely necessary that this coil of distraction create for its victims an unshakeable ground that will become the meaning of our culture. I call that ground of diversion "instant gratification," and the primary form that it assumes in our times is entertainment—all kinds of entertainment, from the arts, to media, movies, television, radio, and now even in the form of pods hung like sacred amulets around the necks of human beings—but more of this later. This drive for instant gratification creates "the entertained democracy." A very brief inventory of some of its effects would include but not be limited to the following. Civic participation is reduced to noisy, enthusiastic rallies, here today and gone tomorrow. Friendship is reduced to a television show that shows how to be friends, what to expect from friends, and even how to be a good friend. Universities spend more and more of their dwindling funds on entertainment possibilities for students even as more and more part-time instructors whose attachment to the institution is marginal are hired to take the place of tenured full-time faculty with solid and deep knowledge that should be imparted to students. Hockey teams, swimming pools, game rooms, basketball and football teams, even the food in the cafeteria are to be touted as incredibly vital "selling points" to registering students. Faculty are told to attend these all-important events so that they can "close the deal." And of course, the reason for these annual college "fairs" is the need to attract more and more students whose tuition has become the driving force behind educational financing. Education is not seen as a necessary public good any more. Appeals to legislators, governors, and influential civic leaders fall on deaf ears. Narrow self-interest and greed are the motivating forces that stifle genuine support. The incessant use of 'exciting' by university administrators is irrefutable evidence of their lack of understanding of what a university education is supposed to be all about.

Something has gone terribly wrong when educational leaders endorse the need to sell their product by burnishing their "brand" through entertainment. The utter lack of Soul shows through and camouflages this disgraceful transformation of one of Soul's most important dwelling places. Expression strong enough to define and condemn this first serpent is no longer available.

The second serpent coils itself around Soul's sense of time and eats into its value. This is the outcome of the dominating influence of the "I" world and the "e" world. Time is swallowed up by these technologies that bore into our lives and scream for attention; that is to say, they distract us. The call is for more and more productivity, the summons to consume more and more of the goods produced. Even the once simple act of communicating by writing is now a daily chore so burdensome that we are given lessens in how to handle our email load because it can cause a drop in our productivity. Much more serious are the myriad and subtle ways in which these forms of cannibalism destroy our sense of expression as a rich and ever-evolving activity that unveils the depths of Soul. A new lingo is out and about, and everyone is using it, but no one is talking about it. I dub it "alphabetic brevity." You know: words that are assembled from alphabetic letters and then used as though everyone knew their meaning. They are used all the time in texting messages, instant messaging, and email. They have spread all over the world, some might say "like wildfire"; some might say it is an "epidemic" or even a "pandemic."

This new language is not to be confused with the tried and true acronyms and clichés that have helped us get through the last century. We have learned to live with them and use them in our speech and in our writing. Most of them sound as though they were made up by some mad Pentagon colonel. No contemporary public or private institution could function without them. But alphabetic brevity is a new breed of cat. It is perfect for functioning in our world of speed and multitasking. But its lasting effect is far more serious and insidious. Like the clichés of our culture, *they stop thinking*. They blunt sharp questions. Once they are used and established as common intellectual property, thinking about their meaning is prohibited. They are just part of the culture and to be used as such. Their meaning and worth are agreed upon even before they are discussed. They are neither icons nor indices nor symbols. They are codes used to accelerate our lines of communication, but these very lines are the lifeblood of Soul. The result of this proliferation of shrunken substitutes for words is mental sclerosis.

I am a university professor, and therefore I experience this second coiling most directly and concretely in my classroom. I find a great fear lurking in my students' minds, especially the freshmen. They fear their future and do not know how things got this way. They fear war and violence and the threat of the nuclear apocalypse. Some of their friends have already died in Iraq. Who is the next to go?

And what caused the present economic catastrophe? What caused the "inconvenient truth" that our planet, our global homeland, is threatened by our very way of life? How did that happen? Why did their elders elect to do nothing? They carry enormous debt just to go to college, which has been taken away from the faculty and is now securely in the hands of "THE MANAGERS" who measure success by student credit hours generated (SCGS) by each classroom teacher. Furthermore, these new technological instruments make all that was private now available for those who know where and how to look. Ipods, email, multitasking, CDs, DVDs, cell phones—one gets the distinct feeling that everything is being monitored. Information overload! The computer lab hums from dawn to dusk. Does anyone ever read a book in a thoughtful manner? One can buy "professionally" crafted papers on the net that have just enough grammatical mistakes to con even the most knowing professor into thinking that this really is the work of the student. Plagiarism is a now common activity.

My students struggle into the classroom bent over by the weight of their text books. The price of these tools of ignorance is obscenely high. And by the way, who is making the profit off all these gadgets now needed to learn? Blackboard, power point presentations, movies, film strips, the claptrap of techno wires, cameras, and TV monitors spread across the classroom. To enter the contemporary classroom these days one must be ready to pick one's way through a jungle of instruments—gimmicks dedicated to the sacred act of learning. Am I really Laocoon?—trapped in the wires surrounding my feet as I seek to reach the blackboard with my simple piece of chalk.

And what is it like in the classroom? Fear lurks. Will I pass? Will I get a high grade? Will my GPA suffer if I take this course? Add in the vanishing job market, and you have a witch's brew worthy of the best horror films. A shrouded feeling of panic pervades the room. It is very difficult to teach in such an atmosphere. Students do not learn well when adrenalin is pumping through their systems.

Last week a student came up to me and asked if she could interview me for the college paper. I said, "On what topic"? She responded, "You have such an unorthodox teaching style, and I think students would like to know about it." I said, "What do you mean, unorthodox?" She said, "You don't use power point or films or even lesson plans, and yet the class moves along with logical order, and we get the substance and the details in a very clear manner." I said, "I have been teaching for forty years, and that's the way I have always taught." She said, "Take my word for it; you're different." Sadly, I had to tell her, "I don't do interviews."

Let me relate another incident. It will help express concretely the current mood of my students. One student in my introductory class came to me after class (we had been discussing war, violence, and justice as laid out in Plato's *Republic*). She said, "I am scared." I tried to point out some good signs, but she interrupted me and said, "But you don't understand, I AM REALLY SCARED!" Who could blame her given the present situation with its collapse of the global economic system and the threat of an ever-spreading war in Pakistan and Afghanistan, the reality of global warning and the gradually emerging truth about the loathsome torture system set up by the previous administration and the way we were lied into the Iraq War. Most of my classes take place in a sullen silence. Questions are rarely asked. I think students are trying to figure out if this whole show is really worth it. There is superior intelligence in my classrooms. I can sense that, but it does not show itself in any engaged way. I can already hear some "manager" telling me that it's my job to engage them. But that's just a not so clever ploy to push responsibility for this culture of poverty and fear onto the backs of the academics. John Kenneth Galbraith in his posthumous book, *Innocent Fraud,* says that the corporation has replaced the other tag lines once used to define economic eras. But this time the corporation has hired managers to direct the business. And when confronted with complaints about unfair situations and policies these managers can say, "I am only enforcing the institution's standards," which is the contemporary equivalent of "I just work here." The fraud is there, and so is the presumed innocence.[3]

Even as time disappears under the weight of information processing (for that is what education has really come down to), another phenomenon has merged. It can be called "Nomadism."[4] In face of the loss of personal identity and a real home within which to settle down and create a sense of self-worth, students have, once again, as in the sixties taken to the road. A simple example shows what I am talking about. Last year I asked a class of some fifty students the following question: "How many of you went to this institution last year?" I was stunned when only twelve students raised their hands. Upon further questioning, it became clear that this generation of college students is quite ready to wander from school to school, as well as from geographical location to geographical location, in order to find or at the very least try to fashion for themselves an education that they can call their own.

In sum the second serpent of distraction culminates in a shocking loss of personal identity. We have had the "Lost Generation," the rebels of the sixties, the Baby Boomers, Generation X, and now we face the results of our cultural irresponsibility. Will Laocoon's children expire? Ironically if they do, it will be because of a loss of time. How can one live in such an environment? Where does one find the strength and grace to withstand the onslaught of diversion and continue onward to forge new values in face of the shipwreck of our present time? "24/7" indeed, demanding incessant multitasking!

The Buddha said all human beings must face the reality of the "Three Poisons" that are always part of human existence. Their styles and forms may change over the centuries, but they are always there bringing sorrow, loss, and even madness. He called these poisons "greed," "hatred," and "delusion." They follow upon one another like the night follows the day. It is precisely at this point that the Second Sign, Mindfulness, appears, the one that provides a way out of the madness that threatens our planet.

It is most appropriate that the first foundation and starting place of this second sign comes from the East. It is Asia that offers us Theravada Buddhism.

MINDFULNESS: THE SECOND SIGN OF THE TIMES

Plato's "Battle of the Giants" has been transformed into a crushing struggle for our attention. This was once a parent's first problem with her children. It has now turned into a major cultural issue. We have moved from the metaphysics of Being and Becoming to the struggle between diversion and mindfulness. But maybe we really are not so far away from Plato's problem; in a previous chapter I cited Plato's answer to this struggle. We are encouraged in the *Sophist* to become like the child and "to say that all that is motionless and in a state of motion are both together that which is and the all."[5] Soul has in it the power to transform what is taken to be real. This is the hypothesis of parents, teachers, psychiatrists, and a host of others committed to the real possibility of reconstructing the worse so that the better may express itself. Despite the seemingly overwhelming power of the great economic and electronic distracters Soul retains this power of restoration. For Soul remains the eloquent amphibian that can express both regions of human experience—the eternal and the temporal.[5] Behind the ideas that are about to be discussed lies the confidence that Soul can bring these two seeming opposites together. Time and its loss are the problems. Put in more traditional language, the expression of the mystical in the temporal is what we now take into account.

I am not unaware of the different attitudes toward mysticism. I have heard it called "a weasel word" (whatever that might mean). New Age devotees to this answer to reality's problems reveal a lack of balance that is also unsettling. Others (especially in philosophy) sneer at its seemingly total absence of meaning. And its oft expressed ineffability seems to drive the last nail in the coffin of any reasonable discussion of mysticism. In the face of these objections, it is necessary to begin with a definition that will be clear, nondenominational, and available to those open to a reasonable approach to this human experience. First, it is only fair and honest to acknowledge the fact that millions of people across the ages of this planet have experienced mystical states.[6]

As a starting point I offer the approach of John Findlay in the chapter entitled "The Logic of Mysticism" in his *Ascent to the Absolute*. I will select what I consider to be the relevant dimensions of his analysis,[7] and urge all to thoroughly read this elegant expression of mysticism as a valid, universally experienced human event:

> I mean by [mysticism] something that shows forth absolutely *every* type of excellence or value in a fashion so transcendent that it can perhaps be said to *be* all these types of excel-

lence than merely to embody or exemplify them, which *is* them all of necessity and is them *together*, and which is certainly the sole cause for their presence in any finite case or contingent manifestation.[8]

A mystical system must not only explain and justify what I may call the unitive aspects of our experience, but also the patent disunity, confusion, imperfection and badness which the world at its surface exhibits.[9]

The subject is so vast, difficult and complex that without a strong, simplifying, personal line, one cannot hope to get any where among its intricacies. I believe that mysticism enters into almost everyone's attitudes, and that it is as much a universal background to experience as the open sky to vision: to ignore it is to be drearily myopic, and to take the element of splendour and depth out of everything, and certainly out of philosophy.[10]

For my purposes the crucial phrase in this definition lies in the words "Without a strong, personal line"; this is in direct harmony with the last chapter's discussion of "masked, practical mystics." Findlay holds that there is a transcendental dimension to human existence. Many of course do not. In fact, there are quite different positions on the question of immanence and transcendence. But they can be put to the side as we pursue the major issue of the signs of the times. By stressing the *personal* choice of those seeking effective mindfulness, the way is opened for any orientation toward practicing this "Second Sign of the Times." I have chosen two masters of mindfulness to oppose the two serpents of diversion. One is the Asian monk Bhante Henepola Gunaratana, and the other is Aaron Beck, the founder of cognitive therapy.[11]

We suffer from a false freedom that assures us it is perfectly acceptable to proclaim as our cultural mantra the word more. Standing opposed to this thoughtless way of life is the counselor, *mindfulness*. I begin its exposition by presenting the work of the Theravada Buddhist monk Bhante Henepola Gunaratana. He has written a most valuable introduction to the experience of *vipassana* meditation. It is called *Mindfulness in Plain English*,[12] a delightful title. But first a word about the man himself. His life is sketched in his *Autobiography*,[13] and it is a most compelling story. I wish to concentrate on a single fact. He was for thirty years a chaplain to the students at American University, and his book is framed to address the very problems we have just been discussing. *Vipassana* is a Pali word that can be translated as "insight." Bhante G. (as he is affectionately called) defines the goal of insight meditation as follows: "The cultivation of the mind toward the aim of seeing in the special way that leads to insight and full understanding."[14]

It is a method to expel distraction from our minds so that we can see the impermanence of the thoughts and desires that either haunt or compel us to act in ways that destroy our sense of what is really real. It is a therapy perfectly suited for the craziness of a world besieged by constant diversion. It has the power to dispel the illusory feelings that destroy our sense of balance. The method is simplicity itself. The meditator assumes a position that demands an upright spine. Other more complicated positions such as the various lotus postures are encouraged but not necessary. Then one begins to breathe. One pays full attention to the feeling of one's breath as it enters and exits the rim of one's nostrils. What inevitably follows is what Buddhists of all persuasions have called "the monkey mind." Here is where Vipassana differs from conventional Western reactions to such thoughts, sensations, and feelings. We have been taught to reject them as evil or obstacles to getting back to the task at hand. In insight meditation, one calmly lets these feelings arise and witnesses them *as they arise and then fall away.*

When this is practiced daily for twenty minutes or so to begin with and then for much longer periods as one progresses in the path to insight, several results follow. We experience the fact that this world and all our feelings, thoughts, and actions in it are impermanent. There is simply nothing, absolutely nothing that will not pass away. The Buddha's emphasis was always on direct experience. He refused to talk about doctrines concerning immanence or transcendence, spirituality or materialism. His response to those who questioned his proposal was also always the same: *Try it!*

It is Soul that will intimately experience the deeply personal fact of the impermanence of the world that so concerns us. This is the first step toward mindfulness as a way of life. There are other results. First, the initial steps toward dismantling the illusions fostered by our ego are taken. Furthermore and most important for this book: mindfulness dispels distraction and gradually restores to mind its power to see things as they really are. With the cessation of distraction the body/mind complex feels greater energy. As lethargy is overcome our interest in our interaction with the world and especially our fellow human beings is suffused with *metta* or loving kindness. We move from the drive for instant gratification to compassion for others. This is no flight from the world; quite to the contrary, it moves Soul toward the world with greater insight, more energy, and more prepared for deeper interactions. Greed is overcome because life as it really is becomes more and more satisfying. Envy dissolves, and hatred of those who we previously thought to have more is shown to be based on nothing substantial. Nothing is permanent. All is in the grip of change.

For all this to happen Soul must be able to experience reality exactly as it is with no fakery, gimmicks, or tricks. The third poison—delusion—can now be met, and Soul dispels it through the clarity gained in *vipassana* practice. This does not happen overnight. The title of the previous chapter, "Soul Work," remains an essential part of the journey. Soul needs "gumption" (to use Bhante G's word) to carry on to the end of its journey. The journey is more like a pilgrimage than just a very long trip. To drive this home I end this brief expression of mindfulness by citing its goals as enumerated by Bhante G: "Our goal is to reach the perfection of all the noble and wholesome qualities latent in our subconscious mind. This goal has five elements to it: purification of mind, overcoming sorrow and lamentation, overcoming pain and grief, treading the path leading to attainment of eternal peace, and attaining happiness by following that path. Keeping this fivefold goal in mind, we can advance with hope and confidence."[15] If you have heard echoes of Spinoza, that is all to the good. No one can claim ownership of the right path. It is not for sale. It is won through direct experience, which takes very hard work.

Cognitive therapy was conceived and formulated by Aaron Beck in 1967 with the publication of his book, *Depression*.[16] Since then, there have been improvements, alterations, and in general a refinement of this method of relieving suffering. Cognitive therapy has taken the planet by storm. It is employed everywhere and under different names with different "founders" claiming authorship. That is a story that someone better versed in the literature is qualified to unfold. I begin by noting its uncanny resemblance to *vipassana* meditation. Both stress the mind, and both look at repetitive negative thinking as something to be dispelled. Like Theravadan meditation the object of the therapy is to let the sufferer encounter and experience the impermanence infecting ingrained habits of mind that have caused such havoc in her life. A fundamental difference is that in cognitive therapy the sufferer is personally guided by a therapist. The nucleus of Beck's therapy can still be found in the last pages of his first book as well as his most recent book, *Schizophrenia*. There is a solid continuity to Beck's work from its beginning to its most recent expression. I begin with the last chapter of *Depression*. Specifically I wish to use chapter 21, "Psychotherapy."[17] First he qualifies his approach by terming it "supportive therapy" with an emphasis on reassurance, ventilation and catharsis, and guidance and environmental change. The causes of the sufferer's pains are almost a mirror image of the Buddha's understanding of the sorrows of human life. The afflictions born by the person in treatment are active but false cognitive patterns. These patterns turn into "automatic thoughts" that the therapy seeks to neutralize and then replace with more humanly wholesome thoughts. In particular the sufferer is lead to distinguish 'ideas' from 'facts.' Then the task of weighing alternative explanations becomes a joint enterprise between therapist and sufferer. Once the basic core of the sufferer's Soul is uncovered, positive transformations can begin to emerge. In line with Spinoza's theory of emotions, there is an affective change when reality replaces delusions. Emotions are necessary for Soul's growth into liveliness. Cognitive therapy involves rigorous work on the part of the sufferer. She must express herself in daily assignments as well as other activities. Soul understood as expression is at the very center of cognitive therapy. This entails actual homework assignments as well as a number of actions meant to move Soul from delusion to reality. Beck describes the process in this way:

> Cognitive psychotherapy . . . postulates that the depressed or depression-prone individual has certain idiosyncratic cognitive patterns (schemas) which may become activated either by specific stresses impinging on specific vulnerabilities or by overwhelming, nonspecific stresses. When the cognitive patterns are activated, they tend to dominate the individual's thinking and to produce the affective and motivational attitudes associated with depression. Cognitive therapy may be used symptomatically during depressions to help the patient gain objectivity toward his automatic reactions and counteract them. During nondepressed periods, the therapy is designed to modify the idiosyncratic cognitive patterns to reduce the patient's vulnerability to future depressions.[18]

The cognitive therapist must prove herself a master of insight, imagination, and intelligence. The sufferer who succeeds in expressing Soul in a healthy way would experience "Loving Kindness," "Compassion," "Appreciative Joy," and "Equanimity," which are the four gifts that *vipassana* meditation promises to those who thoroughly follow that path.

Vipassana's insight therapy seeks to imbue Soul with mindfulness, and so does cognitive therapy. Said as concisely as possible, mindfulness is living in the present moment with the fullest possible awareness of what is going on. To conclude this effort to reconstruct the meaning of Soul in the contemporary world, it can be said that mindfulness is the bridge between spirituality and psychotherapy. Even in the midst of the perpetually perishing, a normative measure can be found. To quote Whitehead: "[S]ouls . . . are the gift from language to mankind"[19] Eloquence arising is the meaning of Soul, and such eloquence has risen once before.

Between 8000 and 200 BCE, there arose an era that Karl Jaspers called "the Axial Age."[20] The historical figures of this age included in China Confucius and Lao-Tse, India saw the rise of the authors of the Vedas and the Upanishads as well as the Buddha. In Iran, Zarathustra created his cosmology of the battle between the forces of light and darkness, and in Palestine there were Elijah, Jeremiah, and Isaiah. Moving toward the west we encounter, among others, Socrates, Plato, and Aristotle. Though different in temperament and message, they shared a common experience, which Jaspers describes as follows:

> The new element in this age is that man everywhere became aware of being as a whole, of himself and his limits. . . . [Human beings] in consciously apprehending [their] limits, set [themselves] the highest aims.

> This era produced the basic categories in which we still think and created the world religions out of which [Souls] still live.

> . . . .

> For the first time there were philosophers. Men who dared to stand on their own feet as individuals. . . . [Human beings] opposed [their] own inwardness to the whole world. [They] discovered in [themselves] the primal source by which [they] might rise above themselves and the world. . . . It was an age of reform.[21]

If at the very dawn of time Soul can rise to its most eloquent expressions and do so in the midst of the most pitiful circumstances, why can it not do the same today?

Jaspers maintains that the age of spirituality was followed by the age of science and technology within which epoch we still live. I propose to take Jaspers seriously but to argue the need for a new axial age. The way out of the distractions that have silenced Soul is to be found in the fact that freedom resides in the human Soul. Furthermore, this freedom can be released through the act of mindfulness.

As I have argued, Spinoza's metaphysics is a metaphysics of identity, not causality. Therefore, what occurs in the body also occurs in the mind, and what occurs in the mind also occurs in the body. When it comes to developing a therapeutics of mindfulness, there is no separation between somatic and psychic acts. The mind/body split that has befuddled philosophy in the contemporary age dissolves and is replaced by the need to develop a theory of action that will unite both aspects within the unity of the human organism.

This attempt to revive Soul as a living force in our world is the last book in a trilogy that began with *Nature: An Environmental Cosmology*, proceeded to *City: An Urban Cosmology*, and now completes itself through this concept of Soul as a force of eloquent expression. In the books *Nature* and *City* the reach and power of Soul lay in the background. Reading this volume as a manifestation of this power, the concept of 'felt intelligence' that played so vital a role in getting in touch with the values inherent in natural and built environments can now be seen as grounded in a spiritual adventure. Where that adventure takes us cannot be known. Human history shows just how good and just how evil eloquence can be. For every Lincoln there is a Hitler. Nevertheless, felt intelligence, especially as understood in the Chinese doctrine of the propensities of things, can encourage us to move toward goodness and away from evil. It is for that reason that I conclude this final chapter with the words of Cormac McCarthy. For just as McCarthy began this chapter with so powerful an insight into our potential for good and for evil, so also he summons up Soul to walk on with hope and dignity and a sense of profound self-worth. I began this final chapter with a quote from Cormac McCarthy and end it with another. The fierce eloquence of those first words is twinned by the words he chose to end his book, and I have selected them to complete this effort to reclaim Soul: "He bowed his head and held his face in his hands and wept. He sat there a long time and after a while the east did gray and after a while the right and godmade sun did rise, once again, for all and without distinction."

EPILOGUE

We have traveled a long distance—from a slave field, through a cosmological account of the structures of Soul, to a plain of eloquence marking the peak of Soul's growth as expression, to the brink of eternity and back, to an invitation to take up Soul work that really matters, to a final confrontation with the signs of our times through meditative practice.

What else remains to be said? I wish to close this effort to reclaim a place for Soul in our times by examining what it means to be a "masked, practical mystic." I also want to bring the Irish brilliance of James Joyce into the conversation. Finally, I will conclude with the most ancient "word-gifts" expressed on our planet. I am speaking of the three gifts bestowed on those who follow Tao.

MASKED, PRACTICAL MYSTICS

The Greek word for mask is *persona*. It is that huge instrument within which an actor would stand and be able to project her voice out into the amphitheater. We are familiar with two of them—that of comedy and tragedy—but there were many others. So a person is hidden because no one can look into our inner selves but our selves. Human persons are withdrawn except for expression. But that is why Soul is expression. But why should a mystic hide herself? Anonymity is the most precious entitlement that a person serious about living a 'mystical' life can possess. Paradoxically, in our fame-driven culture only the mask can bring us fulfillment and happiness.

We have already seen how our culture encourages egotism, individualism, and the personal possession of many, many 'things.' A mask provides a defense against personal desires and against seeking to advertise one's goodness—a fatal move for a Soul that is also seeking authentic expression. How then can we recognize these Soul workers moving about in our world of confusing signs? Jesus gives us the clue: "By their fruits you shall know them" (Matthew 7:15–20). At this time mystics must also be massively practical. That is to say, they must work alongside others and contribute to the common good. Seeking credit for what one has done undoes the act of generosity. As the Irish say: "Self praise, no praise." And what would be the most practical occupation for a masked mystic? Just look around—Souls cry out in pain, despair, and hopelessness. Just listen and then get to work in the most effective way possible.

Remember Wang Yang-ming's insistence on the unity of knowledge and action? To know is to do, but what shall we do? And what shall we say? If you have been meditating along the lines suggested, you will know the true from the false, the genuine for the gimmicky, and the honest from the deceitful. Insight into the human condition is the strength that the masked practical mystic carries into every situation. The traditions we have studied tell us not to worry nor be afraid; if we have been diligent in our practice, what to say and what to do "will be given to you" (Mark 13: 9–13).

Who is a mystic? The most direct response I can give is that a mystic is one who accepts a spiritual realm folded somehow into our everyday lives and is able to experience it mindfully on a daily basis. Experiencing it requires disciplined meditation. I equate meditation and contemplation. And I also include the various kinds of bodywork meant to bring us into direct contact with the spiritual realm: yoga, tai ch'i, breathing exercises, and all other forms of making contact with Soul's real home, goodness. Given our conditions, becoming masked, practical mystics is the most radically powerful action that Soul can undertake.

I have throughout this journey been preoccupied with returning the aesthetic dimension to its rightful place in Soul's structure. I prefer to call it the "domain of feeling." I have also included in it the 'factor of the integer,' which is to say that feeling is intelligent. Where there is measure and proportion, there also is intelligence. What draws feeling forward most intensely is "Beauty." In *The Portrait of the Artist as a Young Man*, James Joyce offers a powerfully evocative and concrete description of the qualities needed to make something beautiful. It sums up in so many ways my effort to fuse feeling and thought and gives Soul some breathing room in this overstuffed world. Using Thomas Aquinas as a place from which to proceed, Joyce says: "Three things are needed for beauty, wholeness, harmony and radiance."[1]

Joyce expands on these qualities of the beautiful. Wholeness is his translation of the Latin *integritas*. We are back in company with

Plato, Spinoza, Neville, and the other friends we have met along the way. Joyce goes on:

> [T]he esthetic image is first luminously apprehended as self-bounded and self-contained upon the immeasurable background of space and time which is not it. You apprehend it as *one* thing. You see it as one whole. You apprehend its wholeness. That is *integritas* [and Whitehead's major form of beauty].
>
> . . . .
>
> You feel the rhythm of its structure. . . . You apprehend it as complex, multiple, divisible, separable, made up of its parts, the result of its parts and their sum, harmonious. That is *consonantia* [and Spinoza's idea of unity].
>
> . . . .
>
> [And what of *claritas*, the last quality?] You see that it is that thing which it is and no other thing. [Here we meet again Duns Scotus and Gerard Manley Hopkins.] The radiance [*claritas*] of which he [Aquinas] speaks is the scholastic *quidditas*, the *whatness* of a thing. This supreme quality is felt by the artist. . . . The mind in that mysterious moment is likened beautifully by Shelley to a fading coal . . . the clear radiance is apprehended luminously by the mind, . . . arrested by its wholeness, and fascinated by its harmony . . . [This experience] is a spiritual state.[2]

Knowledge and feeling unite in the thought of Joyce, Aquinas, Spinoza, Neville, Dun Scotus, and Gerard Manley Hopkins. The echoes of our past work resound through these words. It is enough to listen to them in silence.

Philosophy is the effort to find the appropriate measure for the relation between facts and values. So far our culture has succeeded beyond measure in gathering the facts. But do we know their value? Built into Philosophy's name is the type of effort needed to become wise. Philosophy is NOT wisdom. It is the LOVE of wisdom. After some sixteen years of work, this trilogy reaches its conclusion. Philosophy continues to offer us a daunting task. In a world driven mad by distraction, it is our job to rediscover importance. Mindfulness is the means to experience the direct force of importance.

The *Tao Te Ching* is among the oldest spiritual documents on our planet. Its wisdom is well known. I conclude by using it to set a tone and a direction for our labors:

> I have three Gifts to give.
> Kindness, Simplicity, Patience.[3]

POSTSCRIPT

Though this has been a long and arduous journey, my reader in all likelihood is asking:

> What about immortality?
> What about life after death?
> What about past lives?
> What about out-of-the-body experiences?

I have touched briefly on these issues in certain ways. Neville speaks directly about a "Life of Glory." Spinoza speaks directly about the meaning of the Intellectual Love of God. Grossman translates this expression as the "Spiritual Love of God"[1] and also goes into detail about the difference between "first-order" and "second-order" ideas, by which he means the process of shifting from what you are thinking about and to the process of thinking itself. When we think about thinking, we enter spiritual intuition or the third kind of knowledge (*scientia intuitiva*). In so doing we enter the mind of God insofar as we are able to experience such a "hyper-mind." This occurs when wholes instead of parts, or what can be also termed holism, come into play as a habitual mode of thinking.[2]

However, my response is even more simple and direct. I do not think that any absolute answers can be given to such questions. Reasonable approaches can and have been offered, but that is not the task that I have set for myself. Rather I have tried to give life in this world to the dead word *Soul*. Therefore, this book can be understood as a prolegomenon to such questions. If this is not satisfactory, I ask my reader to consult the selective bibliography as well as the many other sources that have addressed such questions.

NOTES

PRELIMINARIES

1. Joseph Grange, *The City: An Urban Cosmology* (Albany: State University of New York Press, 1999), 235.

INTRODUCTION

1. Kirk and Raven, *The Presocratic Philosophers* (Cambridge: Cambridge University Press, 1957) Fragment 235, p. 205. I translate *logos* as "expression."
2. See Alfred North Whitehead, *Science and the Modern World* (New York: Free, 1967), ch. 3.
3. See Raymond Martin and John Barresi, *The Rise and Fall of the Soul and Self: An Intellectual History of Personal Identity* (New York: Columbia University Press, 2006).
4. See Alfred North Whitehead, *Process and Reality*, corrected edition by Griffin and Sherburne (New York: Free, 1978), 23.
5. David Ray Griffin, *Unsnarling the World Knot* (Berkeley: University of California Press, 1998).
6. The video documentary on American slavery by Ken Burns contains just such a scene. The noted contemporary artist, Veronica Benning, brought it to my attention. Like all great artists the genius of her work resides in her uncanny ability to pick out and express the most meaningful details.
7. Henri Bergson, *An Introduction to Metaphysics* (New York: Bobbs Merrill, 1955), 61.
8. John 1:1.
9. Alfred North Whitehead, *Modes of Thought* (New York: Free, 1968), 60–61.
10. Susanne Langer, *Mind: An Essay on Human Feeling* (Baltimore: Johns Hopkins University Press, 1967), vol. 1, pp. 257–306.
11. Wang Yang-ming, *Instructions for Practical Living*, trans. Wing Tsit-Chang (New York: Columbia University Press, 1963), 10.

12. Neal Grossman, *Healing the Mind: The Philosophy of Spinoza Adapted for a New Age* (London: Associated University Presses, 2003).
13. G. W. F. Hegel, *The Phenomenology of Spirit*, trans. A. V. Miller (Oxford: Oxford University Press, 1977), para. 710.

1. INSCAPE

1. Gerard Manley Hopkins, "As Kingfishers Catch Fire, Dragonflies Draw Flame," in *Poems of Gerard Manley Hopkins*, ed. Robert Bridges (London: Oxford University Press, 1930), 53.
2. See Grange, *Nature*, ch. 4.
3. These concepts are derived from Charles Taylor, *Hegel and Modern Society* (Cambridge: Cambridge University Press, 1979), ch. 1.
4. Rene Descartes, *Meditation II*, and the *Philosophical Writings of Descartes*, vol. 1 trans. Cottingham, Stoothof, and Murdoch (Cambridge: Cambridge University Press, 1985).
5. G. W. F. Hegel, "Preface," the *Phenomenology of Spirit*, trans. Y. Yovel (Princeton: Princeton University Press, 2005), 95.
6. See Charles Darwin, *The Expression of Emotions in Animals* (New York: Philosophical Library, 1872).
7. Alfred North Whitehead, *Modes of Thought* (New York: Free, 1968), 41.
8. Guy Debrock, "Introduction: Process Pragmatism," in *Process Pragmatism*, ed. Guy Debrock (Amsterdam: Rodopi Books, 2006), 1.
9. James A. Austin, M.D., *Zen-Brain Reflections* (Cambridge: MIT Press, 2006) passim; and Alfred North Whitehead, *Process and Reality*, "Creativity, the Category of the Ultimate," 21–22.
10. *Alcoholics Anonymous*, 3d ed. (New York: Alcoholics Anonymous World Services, 1976), 60.
11. Robert Neville, *Boston Confucianism* (New York: State University of New York Press, 2000), 77.
12. This is Iris Murdoch's powerful definition of human knowledge when it achieves its best expression. See her still underappreciated *Metaphysics as a Guide to Morals* (New York: Penguin, 1992), 3.
13. Alfred North Whitehead, *Adventures of Ideas* (New York: Free, 1968), 256.
14. See Robert Neville, *The Cosmology of Freedom* (Albany: State University of New York Press, 1974), ch. 2, for a brilliant analysis of elegance (or in my sense, 'eloquence') as a fundamental normative dimension residing at the heart of Plato's doctrine of participation.
15. See Robert Innis, *Susanne Langer in Focus* (Bloomington: Indiana University Press, 2009), for a superb comprehensive synthesis of all of Langer's prolific scholarly work.
16. Susanne Langer, *Mind: An Essay in Feeling* (Baltimore: Johns Hopkins University Press, 1967). Langer's work merits a full discussion. I am aware

that she would reject my use of soul as derivative from her work. However, I am not convinced that such an employment of her thought is a betrayal of her genius.

17. For example, see David Bohm, *On Creativity* (New York: Routledge, 1996), 98ff.

18. See John Dewey, *Art as Experience* (New York: Capricorn, 1934), passim.

19. Whitehead, *Process and Reality*.

20. Merleau-Ponty's last work is significantly entitled *The Visible and Invisible* and leans heavily on the artist to lead him into his newly arrived at metaphysical vision. The fact that it remained unfinished does not invalidate the power of its title's invocation of the invisible as part of the field of perception. See Merleau-Ponty, *The Visible and the Invisible*, trans. Alphonso Lingis (Chicago: Northwestern University Press, 1968).

21. See Hopkins' beautiful tribute to Duns Scotus, poet philosopher of haeceities, in the poem "Duns Scotus's Oxford." Also view Hopkins' own drawings and sketches for they too reveal his sensitivity to the instresses expressed by the variety of values in the world of nature.

22. Ezekiel xxxvii: 10.

23. See my *John Dewey, Confucius and Global Philosophy* (Albany: State University of New York Press, 2004), ch. 3, "Felt Intelligence."

24. More and more studies come out every day. Later in this study we will make full use of the particular merits of the psychotherapeutic school of "mindfulness therapy."

25. The phrase from the *Politics* is usually translated, "Man is by nature a political animal." The Greek actually reads, "Man is by nature meant to dwell in cities." My translation highlights the social meaning of Aristotle's dictum.

26. G. W. F. Hegel, *The Phenomenology of Spirit*, trans. A. V. Miller (Cambridge: University of Cambridge Press, 1977), 111ff.

2. INVOLVEMENT

1. Alfred North Whitehead, *Science and the Modern World* (New York: Free, 1967), 57.

2. Ibid.

3. Ibid.

4. I would compare this analysis to that of Gerard Edelman who speaks eloquently of neurological patterns, reentrant and degenerate patterns that allow for the brain's plasticity and growth. See *Wider Than the Sky* (New Haven: Yale University Press, 2004), especially the glossary. All of Edelman's books are very well worth reading. The problem I have with his approach is the dismissive way in which he speaks of "spooks" nd "spookiness." He thereby rules out *tout court* any room for soul as an aspect of the human person. He does not seem to recognize that the very term *pattern* is itself one of those invisible "spooks" that he decries. Patterns are actual and can be 'seen' but

even a biologically based theory of the brain must in the end utilize what are actually descendants of Platonic forms to both express and move his argument forward. Patterns are neuronal biological harmonies.

5. See *Nature: An Environmental Cosmology* (Albany: State University of New York Press, 1997), and *The City: An Urban Cosmology* (Albany: State University of New York Press, 1999), passim.

6. Alfred North Whitehead, *Adventures of Ideas* (New York: Free Press, 1967), 256.

7. Ibid., 267.

8. Ibid., 280.

9. Ibid.

10. See Murray Code, *Process, Reality, and the Power of Symbols* (London: Palgrave, 2007), for a comprehensive analysis of the importance of concrete symbols for understanding the reality of process. Also see David Weissman's *Truth's Debt to Value* (New Haven: Yale University Press, 1993) for an erudite and convincing defense of the relation between truth and value.

11. Warren Frisina's *The Unity of Knowledge and Action* (Albany: State University of New York Press, 2002) is a brilliant interpretation of postmodernism's quest for nonrepresentational thinking as a still preliminary inquiry into Wang's much more profound position. His *Instructions for Practical Living* (New York: Columbia University Press, 1963) is required reading for those who would seek to move beyond the stymied intellectualism of deconstruction.

12. See my *John Dewey, Confucius and Global Philosophy*, passim, for a comprehensive analysis of Dewey's theory of experience as environmental interaction aimed at balancing unsettled situations.

13. The "Chang Tsai's Western Inscription," in *A Source Book in Chinese Philosophy*, ed. Wing Tsit Chan (Princeton: Princeton University Press, 1963), 497.

14. Alfred North Whitehead, *Adventures of Ideas*, 281–282.

15. See *The Selected Poetry of Rainer Maria Rilke*, ed. and trans. Stephen Mitchell (New York: Vintage International, 1989), 300. And see Rilke's description of the act of "in-seeing." It is a perfect enactment of Hopkins' "inscape," 313.

3. FEELING THE ALTERNATIVE

1. *Process and Reality*, 161.
2. See Ralph Pred, *Onflow* (Cambridge: MIT Press, 2005), ch. 6.
3. See *Adventures of Ideas*, chs. 16, 17, and 18.
4. See ibid., ch. 17.
5. See ibid., chs. 16, 17, and 18.
6. See ibid., 266.
7. The origins of this indifference to other humans are captured with stunning clarity in John Kenneth Galbraith's last publication: *The Econom-*

ics of Innocent Fraud: Truth for Our Time (New York: Houghton Mifflin, 2004). It contains within its brief sixty-two pages a world of wisdom that shows how the corporation nullifies all sense of guilt and at the same time muffles dissent.

8. See ch. 2, note 4.

9. Strangely enough, after I had thought through and expressed my ideas on "poise," I began reading Robert Neville's *Religion in Late Modernity* (Albany: State University of New York Press, 2002) and found in the index the following entry concerning "poise, pp. 179–83; defining self, 42–44." He also uses the finite/infinite contrast that is part of the theory of awareness that I am working out in this chapter. I have read and learned a great deal from all of Neville's work, but I never read this material on poise. There is a shocking similarity. How so? Who knows? Maybe we are both onto something.

10. Taken from the Bob Dylan tour blog.

11. I am, of course, using John Dewey's description of the heart and soul of experience.

12. Deng, Ming-Dao, *Everyday Tao* (San Francisco: HarperCollins, 1996), 44.

13. See my *Nature, and The City,* passim, and the detailed discussion in *John Dewey, Confucius, and Global Philosophy* (Albany: State University of New York Press, 2004),ch. 2, "Felt Intelligence."

14. I borrow the phrase from Francois Jullien's brilliant book, *The Propensity of Things* (New York: Zone Books, 1995).

15. The classic presentation of this act of experience is the first chapter of John Dewey's, *Art as Experience* (New York: Capricorn, 1934). It is also precisely what Alfred North Whitehead means by the phrase "the withness of the body." The concept is scattered throughout his writings, but its most sustained treatment is to be found in *Process and Reality*, part 4.

4. ELOQUENCE ARISING

1. Alfred North Whitehead, *Science and the Modern World* (New York: Free, 1968), 131.

2. Charles S. Peirce, *The Collected Papers of Charles S. Peirce,* ed. Hartshorne and Weiss (Cambridge: Harvard University Press, 1931-1938) vol. 5: 315. Hereafter cited as CP followed by the volume number and then the paragraph number.

3. Charles S. Peirce, "A Guess at the Riddle" in the *Essential Peirce*, ed. Houser and Kloesel (Bloomington: Indiana University Press, 1992) 1, 248.

4. James Joyce, *Ulysses* (New York: Vintage International Edition, 1990), 34.

5. Alfred North Whitehead, *Science and the Modern World*, 101.

6. CP 1: 356.

7. CP 2: 297.

8. Plato, *The Sophist*, trans. Nicholas P. White (Indianapolis: Hackett, 1993), 249.

9. See Donald Verene's masterful study of the images in the *Phenomenology of Spirit: Hegel's Recollection* (Albany: State University of New York Press, 1985).

10. See the *Tao Te Ching* no. 2.

11. Alfred North Whitehead, *Adventures of Ideas*, 267.

12. Ibid.

13. See T. P. Kasulis's eloquent discussion of Zen and human identity, in *Zen Action, Zen Person* (Honolulu: University of Hawaii Press, 1985). *Mu* is the Japanese word for "nothing."

14. Alfred North Whitehead, *Science and the Modern World*, 93.

15. I emphasize lost souls because it is title of David Weissman's compelling study of the effects of dualism in our culture. See David Weissman, *Lost Souls* (Albany: State University of New York Press, 2006).

16. Immanuel Kant, *The Critique of Pure Reason*, trans. Werner S. Pluhar (Indianapolis: Hackett, 1996.), B 103–15.

17. Murray Code, *Process, Reality and the Power of Symbols: Thinking With A. N. Whitehead* (New York: Palgrave Macmillan, 2007).

18. Ralph Pred, *Onflow* (Cambridge: MIT Press, 2005).

19. Karen Horney, *Self-Analysis* (New York: Norton, 1942), 264.

20. Karen Horney, *The Neurotic Personality of Our Time* (New York: Norton, 1937).

21. Alfred North Whitehead, *Adventures of Ideas*, 275.

22. He borrows the term from Coleridge, whose insistence upon the importance of imagination for a full human life forms the backbone of Code's analysis of the "Power of Symbols."

23. Symposium, 200.

24. T. S. Eliot, *The Wasteland*, 423–24.

5. ETERNAL AND TEMPORAL CONTRASTS

1. Robert Neville, *Eternity and Time's Flow* (Albany: State University of New York Press, 1993), xvii.

2. Ibid., 12–13.

3. Ibid., 115, 118.

4. Ibid., 119.

5. Ibid.

6. Ibid., 118.

7. Lao-Tzu, *Tao Te Ching*, trans. Stephen Addiss and Stanley Lombardo (Indianapolis: Hackett, 1993), no. 1.

8. Susanne Langer, *Mind: An Essay on Human Feeling* (Baltimore: Johns Hopkins Press, 1967) vol. 1, part 3, "*Natura Naturans*," chapter 8, 261.

9. As the above citation shows, this critical moment in Langer's work is precisely where she introduces her key concept of "the act." It is not by

accident that she precedes this chapter by making "the act" the pivot around which the transmutation of feeling into mind is to be understood.

10. But see Neville's favorable comments on Spinoza, *Eternity and Time's Flow*, 146, where Neville says, "[H]is (Spinoza's) is not pantheism at all but one rather like that defended in this book to account for eternity and time's flow. Spinoza, however, was not friendly to the radical contingency implied in creation *ex nihilo*." I maintain that when Spinoza defines substance and attributes in *Ethics*, part 1, definitions 3 and 4 he is saying that substance (or the source of the whole of reality, or God or Nature) can only be conceived in and through itself, he is saying something very much like Neville's God unknown before creation. I also maintain that Spinoza's definition of attributes as "that which the intellect perceives of substance as constituting its essence" adds to my argument. Far better to call Substance or God or Nature, "X,' the unknown, which is *causa sui* and therefore unknowable in advance of its creative activity.

11. This is not to say that Neville and Langer lack concreteness. Indeed both studies make use of concrete applications and examples of the relevance of their views to human life and its destiny. I am using Spinoza because I maintain that soul is intimately tied to its emotional life, and Spinoza has done the best job so far of weaving human emotions into a metaphysics.

12. Baruch Spinoza, the *Ethics*, trans. Samuel Shirley (Indianapolis: Hackett, 1982), part 1, explication 8. All translations are taken from this volume.

13. See ibid., explication 7.

14. Murray Code, *Process, Reality and the Power of Symbols: Thinking with Whitehead* (New York: Palgrave, 2007), passim. See also Code, *Myths of Reason: Vagueness, Rationality and The Lure of Logic* (New Jersey: Humanities, 1995). His reservations about forms of empirical science and the ultimacy of mathematics as the primal mode of epistemological certainty were first worked out in *Organism and Order* (Albany: State University of New York Press, 1985), which showed how Whitehead's philosophy of science and mathematics preserves the importance of these disciplines even as it demonstrates their limitations.

15. A terrifying account of what it means to lose involvement is to be found in Sandy Hartman, *Lose Your Mother: A Journey along the Atlantic Slave* (New York: Farrar, Straus, and Giroux, 2007).

16. *Ethics*, part 4, proposition 7.

17. *Ethics*, part 4, proposition 11.

18. *Ethics*, part 2, definition 6. "By reality and perfection I understand the same thing."

19. *Ethics*, part 2, proposition 7.

20. *Ethics*, part 5, proposition 24.

21. *Ethics*, part 2, propositions 40, scholium 2.

22. *Ethics*, part 2, proposition 40, scholium 3.

23. The full meaning of "mindful" will become evident later when Vipassana meditation as taught by Theravada Buddhism and Aaron Beck's cognitive therapy are discussed.

130 / Notes to Chapter 6

24. *Ethics*, part 3, proposition 25 and demonstration.
25. *Ethics*, part 3, definition of the emotions, 6.
26. *Ethics*, part 1, proposition 15.
27. *Ethics*, part 5, proposition 39, scholium 2.
28. *Ethics*, part 5, proposition 42, scholium.
29. *Ethics*, part 4, proposition 67.
30. *Ethics*, part 5, propositions 21–42; *Eternity and Time's Flow*, part 4, "Eternal Life."
31. This is my translation. I believe that Spinoza is really talking about a "belly laugh," the kind that can double us over and even be painful. It is what the Italians call *"boffo."*

6. SOUL WORK

1. Thomas Merton's *Inner Experience*, ed. William Shannon (New York: Harper, 2003), is a reworked version of material left incomplete at his death. The editor tells us that it was supposed to be a definitive revision of his earlier *What Is Contemplation?* (Springfield IL: Templegate, 1981). Jacques Maritain wrote Merton about that work and pointed out that Merton's phrase "quasi-contemplatives" did not fully express the undertaking of those who continue to work in the everyday world and sustain a practice of meditation. He suggested the phrase "masked contemplatives," which Merton agreed was much more appropriate. See *The Inner Experience*, 162, note 19. Because Merton (and Maritain) were concerned about active work in the world, and because I have committed myself to Wang-yang Ming's dictum concerning the unity of knowledge and action, I have taken the liberty of placing the word "practical" in between "masked contemplatives." Also since this volume uses mystical" to discuss certain aspects of soul work, I have used "mystic" to replace contemplatives. Becoming a "masked practical mystic" is the soul's calling at this time in human history. The search for better expressions is in accord with the message of this book.

2. In coming to this understanding of the most important expression in the *Ethics* I have been helped immeasurably by the work of Paul Wienpahl, *The Radical Spinoza* (New York: New York University Press, 1979), 58. Besides pointing out that this definition expresses what I also have been trying to express throughout this work, Wienpahl also has identified the central idea driving Spinoza's systematic thinking: UNITY. In this definition Wienpahl points out that *"constantem"* is derived from *consto* among whose many meanings is "arising." In addition, he cites the fact that Spinoza uses the same exact word with the same connotation in the *Tractatus Theologico-Politicus* (20). None of the extant English translations has picked up this insight. When joined to the Neoplatonic tradition of understanding theophanic expression as the cement that holds the evolving universe together, a novel and bright light is thrown on the *Ethics* and its contemporary meaning. Reaching as far back as the participation theory of Plato and the teaching of Plotinus that the cause remains active within

the effect, much of the mystery of Spinoza's 'mysticism' dissolves. I continue to be troubled by the complete absence of reference to Wienpahls's work among the most diligent and important contemporary Spinoza scholars.

3. My translation owes much to Wienpahl but equally as much to my study of the theophanic tradition in both Eastern and Western philosophy. See the recently published *Theophany* by Eric D. Perl for a masterly exposition of this philosophic tradition. I have tried to express the depth and reach of this tradition in "An Irish Tao," in *Tao & God, the Journal of Chinese Philosophy* [Special Edition edited by Joseph Grange] 29, no. 1. Spinoza's philosophy is an inexhaustible resource for comparative philosophy.

4. *Ethics*, part 2, proposition 40, scholium 2.

5. Ibid.

6. *Ethics*, part 1, proposition 18.

7. *Ethics*, part 3, proposition 11.

8. *Ethics*, part 4, appendix.

9. As noted before, this is the brilliant expression adopted by Neal Grossman in his groundbreaking work, *Healing the Mind: The Philosophy of Spinoza Adapted for a New Age*. He uses it as a synonym for Substance, God or Nature as he works through Spinoza's philosophy in a most illuminating manner. He makes a powerful case for its practical value in our alienated age. Along with Wienphal's previously cited work, this study turns on its head all interpretations that dismiss Spinoza's work as hopelessly hyper-rational. Grossman demonstrates the remarkable therapeutic power of Spinoza's vision of unity and wholeness.

10. *Ethics*, part 4, proposition 52, scholium.

11. *Ethics*, part 3, definition 28.

12. Ibid., definition 26.

13. These definitions are taken from the "Definitions of the Emotions" that end part 3 of the *Ethics*.

14. Note the similarity between this emotion and Neville's concept of a life of glory as described in *Eternity and Time's Flow*, part 4.

15. What follows are paraphrases from *Ethics*, part 4, propositions 67–73.

16. See my presidential address to the Metaphysical Society of America. Entitled "The Generosity of the Good," it spells out the oft forgotten dimension of Plato's Good; namely, that the Good gives and in that giving resides all the power and strength that being has and knowledge receives. *The Review of Metaphysics*, 62, no. 1: 111–21.

17. *Ethics*, part 4, proposition 46, scholium.

18. Once again, the similarity between this emotion and Neville's concept of a life of glory in *Eternity and Time's Flow* is striking. Both thinkers insist on the reality of eternity and the theme of glory understood as an outcome of this reality.

19. See Neal Grossman, *The Healing of the Mind*, 133.

20. Spinoza's development of this theme takes place with breathtaking speed in propositions 25 through 36.

21. See the *de Emendatione Intellectus* (1). As expressed earlier, in my judgment this mysterious but powerful early work is best translated as "the Healing of the Mind." Note the beginning "to find out . . . whether there was something which . . . would *continuously* give me the greatest *joy*, to *eternity*" (my emphases).

22. *Ethics*, part 5, proposition 20.

23. Recall the earlier discussion of Neville's conception of eternity and a life of glory.

24. *Ethics*, part 5, proposition 42, scholium.

25. See Neal Grossman, *Healing the Mind*.

26. *The Confessions*, book 9.

27. See Wang Yang-ming, passim.

28. Donald Davidson, "Spinoza's Causal Theory of the Affects," in *Desire and Affect*, ed. Yirmiyahu Yovel (New York: Little Room, 1999), 99.

29. Marx Wartofsky, "Action and Passion," in *Spinoza: A Collection of Critical Essays*, ed. Majorie Grene (Garden City, NY: Anchor Books, 1973), 349.

30. *The Way of Chuang Tzu*, trans. Thomas Merton (Boston: Shambala, 1965) 54–55.

31. The phrase is taken from Murrray Code. See his two recent works cited in the previous chapter. His insights can aid us in breaking free from our bewitchment with scientism.

32. Hegel, "The Beautiful Soul," 383 et. seq.

33. *Ethics* 5, proposition 42.

7. SIGNS OF THE TIMES

1. *Sophist*, 245–49.

2. *Aeneid*, book 2, 47 et.seq. *"Timeo Danaos ET dona ferentes."*

3. John Kenneth Galbraith, *The Economics of Innocent Fraud: Truth for Our Time* (Boston: Houghton Mifflin, 2004). This slim volume is Galbraith's last work, and it distills in sixty-two pages a lifetime of reflection on the ways economic systems dictate the cultural forms that beleaguer soul's effort to express the values that really matter. Galbraith's work is a stunning example of what I mean by "eloquence arising."

4. This, of course is the title of Deleuze's small book on what is happening in our culture, *Nomadism*.

5. *Sophist*, 249D. To use a more homely example Plato is obviously referring to the "wisdom of the child" who when offered a choice between ice cream and cake, responds automatically: "Both!"

6. See William James, *The Varieties of Religious Experience* (New York: Routledge, 2002) [Centennial Edition], for a prolific descriptive collection of mystical experiences undergone by souls in the last century.

7. John Findlay, "The Logic of Mysticism," in *The Ascent to the Absolute* (New York: Humanities, 1970), 172–83.

8. Ibid., 180.
9. Ibid., 181.
10. Ibid., 182–83.
11. I owe appreciation and knowledge of these two spiritual therapies to my wife, Claudine Grange, PMH-NP, whose expert use of these ways of achieving a balanced life has helped her patients, our family, and herself and myself.
12. Bhante Henepola Gunaratana, *Mindfulness in Plain English* (Boston: Wisdom, 2002). Also definitely relevant are his two other works: *Eight Mindful Steps to Happiness* (Boston: Wisdom, 2001) and *Journey to Mindfulness: The Autobiography of Bhante G.* (Somerville, MA: Wisdom, 2003).
13. Gunaratana Henepola, *Autobiography of Bhante G.*, passim.
14. Gunaratana Henepola, *Mindfulness*, 33.
15. Ibid., 50.
16. Aaron Beck, *Depression* (New York: Harper and Row, 1967), 311–32; Beck also refers the reader to chs. 17 and 18 where he outlines the theory of cognitive therapy.
17. Ibid., 318.
18. Alfred North Whitehead, *Modes of Thought* (New York: Free, 1968), 41
19. Karl Jaspers, *The Way to Wisdom* (London: Yale University Press, 1954), 98ff.
20. Ibid., 99–101.
21. Cormac McCarthy, *The Crossing* (New York: Vintage, 1995), 426.

POSTSCRIPT

1. He also discusses out-of-the-body experiences as empirical corroboration of what occurs when the body is eliminated as a factor in consciousness. See Grossman, 49, 51, 113, 223.
2. Ibid., ch. 4, "Freedom from Bondage," 155–211, especially pp. 167–74.

EPILOGUE

1. James Joyce, *Portrait of the Artist as a Young Man* (New York: Viking, 1964), 211–13.
2. Ibid.
3. *Tao Te Ching*, no. 67, my translation.

SELECTED BIBLIOGRAPHY

The literature on the relations, if any, among soul, brain, and mind is vast and grows more so each day. This bibliography reflects that fact in the following ways. I list certain anthologies that contain the more important articles that have appeared in the last ten or so years. Each provides authors who take up different approaches to the subject matter and reflect different points of departure in analyzing the subject matter. Even here, my selections may appear out of date. Consider the fact that a recent catalogue from Oxford University Press advertises two 'new' handbooks—one for the Philosophy of Mind with more than 45 subdivisions and 680 pages and one for philosophy and neuroscience that lists 24 subdivisions and is 752 pages.

The anthologies are very useful since they divide the subject matter into a number of different sections depending on the approaches taken. This provides a very useful orientation to the field. For the sake of the reader, I have reduced the list to a manageable three that represent classic and contemporary approaches to the subject matter. Even so, I am sure that I omitted some important authors and approaches. Following these anthologies, I provide a list of books that I, for a variety of reasons, have found helpful, interesting, supportive, or opposed to the position I have presented. The list of authors is by no means exhaustive. I encourage those interested to use the bibliographies provided by each of these authors. I have appended remarks to this list of selected authors in order to help the reader orient herself or himself around a dizzying realm that is sometimes science, sometimes philosophy, sometimes spiritual, and sometimes all three at the same time. Such an approach will broaden and deepen one's knowledge of this most important subject. It may also justify the use of the term *jungle* in my introductory remarks.

ANTHOLOGIES

Chalmers, David. *Philosophy of Mind*. Oxford: Oxford University Press, 2002.
Hameroff, Stuart, Alfred Kasniak, and Alwyn Scott. *Toward a Science of Consciousness II*. Cambridge: MIT Press, 1998.
Heil, John. *Philosophy of Mind*. Oxford: Oxford University Press, 2004.

* * *

Alper, Matthew. *The God Part of the Brain*. Naperville, Illinois: Sourcebooks, 2008. [A scientific interpretation of human spirituality and God.]
Augustine, St. *The Confessions*. Translated by Maria Boulding, O.S.B. New York: Vintage, 1977. [Brilliant contemporary translation of the classic spiritual autobiography.]
Austin, James, M.D. *Zen and the Brain*. Cambridge: MIT Press, 1998. [A rightly praised classic that uses Zen meditative experience to explore the width and depth of consciousness.]
———. *Zen-Brain Reflections*. Cambridge: MIT Press, 2006. [The author's follow up discussion of the issues raised in his first work.]
Barnard, G. William. *Exploring Unseen Worlds*. Albany: State University of New York Press, 1997. [Excellent student of James' research on consciousness.]
Barnhardt, Bruno. *The Future of Wisdom*. New York: Continuum, 2008.
Beauregard Mario, and Denyse O'Leary. *The Spiritual Brain*. New York: Harper, 2007. [A fascinating argument from neurology for the existence of the soul.]
Beck, Aaron. *Depression*. New York: Harper, 1967. [The pioneering work that began the mindfulness cognitive therapy movement.]
Bermudez, Marcel, editor. *The Body and the Self*. Cambridge: MIT Press, 1995. [A still valuable collection of essays examining the basic questions of brain, soul, and self.]
Brook, Andrew, and Robert Stainton. *Knowledge and Mind*. Cambridge: MIT Press, 2001. [An introductory text that deals with both the epistemology and the philosophy of mind.]
Brown, Warren, Nancey Murphy, and H. Newton Malony, editors. *Whatever Happened to the Soul?* Minneapolis: Fortress, 1998. [A still relevant anthology of articles arguing for the scientific importance of the spiritual dimension.]
Brown, Peter. *Augustine of Hippo*. Berkeley: University of California Press, 1967. [The classic biography.]
Bulkeley, Kelly. *Soul, Psyche, Brain*. New York: Palgrave, 2005. [A stimulating study of the cutting edge issues that span science, religion, and spirituality at the beginning of the new millennium.]
———. *The Wondering Brain*. New York: Routledge, 2005. [A balanced portrait of how cognitive neuroscience and religion can help each other enter deeper into the mystery of the mind.]

Callahan, Annice, RSCJ. *Spiritual Guides for Today*. New York: Crossroad, 1992. [Though written almost twenty years ago, the figures portrayed in this volume demonstrate the continuing relevance of regarding soul as a real entity influencing our lives.]

Chalmers, David. *The Conscious Mind*. Oxford: Oxford University Press, 1996. [One of the most respected philosophers of mind puts forth his theory.]

Clarke, D. S, *Panpsychism and the Religious Attitude*. Albany: State University of New York Press, 2003. [A philosopher defends panpsychism as an alternative to mechanism and humanism.]

Clayton, Philip. *Mind and Emergence*. New York: Oxford University Press, 2004. [A carefully written analysis of the case for the emergence of mind as an important possibility in science and the philosophy of mind.]

Code, Murray. *Myths of Reason*. New Jersey: Humanities, 1995.

———. *Order and Organism*. State University of New York Press, 1985.

———. *Process, Reality, and the Power of Symbols, Thinking with A. N. Whitehead*. New York: Palgrave, 2007.

Colapietro, Peter. *Peirce's Approach to the Self*. Albany: State University of New York Press, 1989.

Coward, Harold. *The Perfectibility of Human Nature in Eastern and Western Thought*. Albany: State University of New York Press, 2008. [A superb guide to what is possible for human beings according to the teachings of the major Eastern and Western religions.]

Crabbe, James, editor. *From Soul to Self*. New York: Routledge, 1999. [A concise collection of clear essays dealing with the most important questions in philosophy, theology, and science.]

Csikszentmihalyi, M. *Flow*. New York: Harper, 1993. [A noted psychologist presents "steps toward enhancing the quality of life."]

Curley, Edwin, translator. *The Collected Works of Spinoza*. Princeton: Princeton University Press, 1985. [The most recent translation and commentary on Spinoza's philosophy.]

Damasio, Antonio. *The Feeling of What Happens*. New York: Harcourt, 1999. [Damasio is the leading figure in the relatively new field of neurophilosophy. As a neuroscientist, he is a materialist. His books are written with verve and clarity.]

D'Aquili, Eugene, and Andrew Newberg. *The Mystical Mind*. Minneapolis: Fortress, 1999. [This readable book probes the biology of the religious experience.]

Deck, John, *Nature, Contemplation, and the One*. New York: Larson, 1991. [The best concise introduction to one of the greatest philosophers of soul.]

Edelman, Gerald. *Bright Air, Brilliant Fire*. New York: Basic Books, 1992.

———. *Wider Than the Sky*. New Haven: Yale University Press, 2004. [Edelman is a Nobel Prize winner and the author of many important, elegantly written, and intriguing books in the growing field of neurophilosophy. He is a convinced materialist.]

Ellwood, Robert. *Mysticism and Religion*. New York: Seven Bridges, 1999. [A thorough account of mystical experience, both past and present.]
Evans, Donald. *Spirituality and Human Nature*. Albany: State University of New York Press, 1993. [An excellent examination of the sweep of experience involved in human spirituality.]
Fields, Gregory. *Religious Therapeutics*. Albany: State University of New York Press, 2001. [An examination of the relation between psychophysical health and spiritual health in Yoga, Ayurveda, and Tantra.]
Findlay, J. N. *Ascent to the Absolute*. New York: Humanities, 1970. [The classic text of one of America's leading idealist philosophers.]
Flanagan, Owen. *The Problem of the Soul*. New York: Basic Books, 2002. [An authoritative study of the major issues in the philosophy of mind.]
Forman, Robert, editor. *The Innate Capacity*. New York: Oxford University Press, 1998. [A superb collection of essays that argue that mysticism is an innate human capacity].
———. *Mysticism, Mind, Consciousness*. Albany: State University of New York Press, 1999. [A thorough analysis of mysticism, especially the thesis that such experiences involve a form of knowledge by identity with the object known.]
Fox, Matthew. Commentator. *Breakthrough: Meitser Eckhart's Creation Spirituality in New Translation*. New York: Image Books, 1980. [Comprehensive analysis of the long forgotten and oft condemned Rhineland mystic.]
Grange, Joseph. *The City an Urban Cosmology*. Albany: State University of New York Press, 1999. [Using the cosmological method to display the values of city life.]
———. "The Generosity of the Good." *The Review of Metaphysics* 62, no. 1 [Presidential Address to the Metaphysical Society of America dealing with the major themes of soul.]
———. "An Irish Tao." In *Tao and God* [Special Edition of *The Journal of Chinese Philosophy* 29, no. 1, March 2002] edited by Joseph Grange. [A comparative analysis of divine causality as expressed in classical Taoism and the Neoplatonic philosophy of John Scotus Eriugena.]
———. *John Dewey, Confucius, and Global Philosophy*. Albany: State University of New York Press, 2004. [Comparative philosophy that utilizes 'felt intelligence' as a key concept to bring Asian and American philosophy together.]
———. "The Lotus Sutra and Whitehead's Last Writings," *Journal of Chinese Philosophy* 28. 2001. [Exploring Upaya ('skillful soul tools') from Asian and process perspectives.]
———. *Nature: An Environmental Cosmology*. Albany: State University of New York Press, 1997. [An articulation of the cosmological method and its significance for reforming environmental ethics.]
———. "Zhuangzi's Tree." *The Journal of Chinese Philosophy* 32, no. 2. June 2005. [Using a Taoist master's famous tree discourse to bring out the process of goodness inherent in every entity.]

Griffin, David. *Unsnarling the World Knot*. Berkeley: University of California Press, 1998. [The premier defense of the process position on mind-body interaction based on the philosophy of Alfred North Whitehead.]

Grossman, Neal. *Healing the Mind*. London: Associated Universities Press, 2003. [A brilliant adaptation of Spinoza's *Philosophy for Our Age*. As highly recommended as Gunaratana's work.]

Gunaratana, Bhante Henepola. *Mindfulness in Plain English*. Boston: Wisdom, 2002. [A Theravada Buddhist master provides the most lucid guide yet to Vipassana meditation, truly a gold mine.]

Happold, F. C. *Mysticism*. New York: Penguin, 1963. [Most highly recommended as a place to start on a journey toward understanding mystical experience.]

Hasker, William. *The Emergent Self*. Ithaca: Cornell University Press, 1999. [Excellent comparative study of consciousness that employs both neuroscience and challenges to contemporary forms of dualism.]

Inchausti, Robert. *The Ignorant Perfection of Ordinary People*. Albany: State University of New York Press, 1991. [Sterling accounts of how soul has transformed our contemporary culture.]

Innis, Robert. *Susanne Langer in Focus: The Symbolic Mind*. Bloomington: Indiana University Press, 2009. [An incisive and comprehensive analysis of the major works of Susanne Langer whose research constitutes a signal contribution to the biological, cultural, and philosophical study of mind in nature.]

Jaynes, Julian. *The Origin of Consciousness in the Breakdown of the Bicameral Mind*. Houghton Miflin, 1978. [A neglected but still very relevant study of the human mind from its origin to its present state.]

Johnson, Mark. *The Body in the Mind*. Chicago: University of Chicago Press, 1987. [A pioneering study of how the body and the mind use language to experience the world.]

Johnson, Steven. *Mind Wide Open*. New York: Scribner, 2004. [The author is a journalist who brings great lucidity and even humor to the questions emerging concerning the materialist basis of neuroscience.]

Jones, Richard. *Mysticism and Morality*. New York: Lexington Books, 2004. [A study of the intersections among, ethics, spirituality, and science].

Kant, Immanuel. *The Critique of Pure Reason*. Translated by Norman Kemp Smith. London: Macmillan, 1929.

Keating, Thomas. *Open Mind, Open Heart*. Rockport, MA.: Element, 1986. [A Trappist monk's effort to recover the Christian contemplative heritage.]

Lakoff, George, and Mark Johnson. *Philosophy in the Flesh*. New York, 1999. [Two leading philosophers argue that the findings of neuroscience require a radical rethinking of what it means to be human. This book should be required reading for every philosophy student.]

Ledoux, Joseph. *The Emotional Brain*. New York: Simon and Schuster, 1996. [A scientific explanation of the origin and place of emotions.]

Lovejoy, Arthur. *The Revolt against Dualism.* LaSalle, Illinois: Open Court, 1960. [The book that began the historical investigation of our present dilemmas.]

Maritain, Jacques. "*Todo y Nada.*" In *The Degrees of Knowledge* (New York: Charles Scribners' Sons, 1932). [The brilliant concluding chapter on the relation of metaphysics and mysticism.]

Marrone, Robert. *Body of Knowledge.* Albany: State University of New York Press, 1990. [An introduction to body/mind psychology.]

Martin, Raymond, and John Barresi, *The Rise and Fall of Soul and Self.* New York: Columbia University Press, 2006. [An intellectual history of personal identity.]

McCarthy, Cormac. *All the Pretty Horses.* New York: Vintage, 1992. [An award-winning use of fiction to express the soul in its will power, courage, strength, and despair, among other qualities.]

———. *The Crossing.* New York: Vintage, 1994. [Volume 2 of *The Border Trilogy*, even more compelling than the first.]

Meisner, W. W., S. J., M. D. *Psychoanalysis and Religious Experience.* New Haven: Yale University Press, 1984. [A still provocative study of connections between the unconscious and religious experience.]

Merton, Thomas. *The Inner Experience.* San Francisco: Harper, 2003. [A practical guide to meditation by American Catholicism's most important master of mystical contemplation.]

Murdoch, Iris. *The Sovereignty of the Good.* London: Routledge and Kegan Paul, 1970. [A singular study of the relations among soul, happiness, and goodness].

Murphy, Nancey. *Bodies, Souls, or Spirited Bodies.* New York: Cambridge University Press, 2006. [A vigorous defense of the spiritual dimension.]

Neville, Robert C. *Eternity and Time's Flow.* Albany: State University of New York Press, 1993. [An indispensable account of the dynamic relations between the eternal and the temporal regions affecting soul.]

———. *Symbols of Jesus.* Cambridge: University of Cambridge Press, 2001. [Contains a very clear and compressed account of the material discussed in *Eternity and Time's Flow.*]

Newberg, Andrew, Eugene D'Aquili, and Vincent Rause, *Why God Won't Go Away.* New York: Ballantine Books, 2001. [Qualified medical researchers argue for the existence of God as a natural part of brain processes.]

Olthuis, James, editor. *Knowing Otherwise.* New York: Fordham University Press, 1997. [Examines the borders between philosophy and spirituality.]

Ostrow, Mortimer. *Soul, Mind, and Brain.* New York: Columbia University Press, 2007. [An empirical based psychoanalytic study of spiritual phenomena and contemporary brain science.]

Otto, Rudolf. *Mysticism East and West* New York: Macmillan, 1932. [One of the pioneering efforts to do comparative mystical philosophy.]

Plotinus, translated by Stephen MacKenna. *The Enneads.* New York: Larson, 1922. [The classic contemplative study of soul in late antiquity.]

Pols, Edward. *Mind Regained.* Ithaca: Cornell University Press, 1998. [A masterful and completely accessible presentation of the issues involved

in our cultural obsession with reductive science at the expense of the experience of mind itself.]
Pred, Ralph. *Onflow: The Dynamics of Consciousness and Experience*. Cambridge: MIT Press, 2005. [A splendid analysis of consciousness as developed in the philosophical tradition of American naturalism.]
Ratey, John. *Spark*. New York: Little, Brown, 2008. [The relation between exercise and mental and emotional states.]
Rosenberg, Gregg. *A Place for Consciousness*. New York: Oxford University Press, 2004. [An original contribution to the relation between mind and causation.]
Roy, Louis, O. P. *Mystical Consciousness*. Albany: State University of New York Press, 2003. [A comparative study of western and Japanese mystical experiences].
Searle, John. *Mind*. New York: Oxford University Press, 2004. [A clear introduction to this eminent thinker's philosophy of mind.]
———. *The Rediscovery of the Mind*. Cambridge: MIT Press, 1992. [The dean of American philosophy of mind reviews his work and proposes some important revisions.]
Shaviro, Steven. *Without Criteria*. Cambridge: MIT Press, 2009. [A very compelling response to the question, What if Whitehead had replaced Martin Heidegger as the century's most influential thinker?]
Shusterman, Richard. *Body Consciousness*. Cambridge: Cambridge University Press, 2008. [An American philosopher extends the tradition of American naturalism through an inquiry into the body and consciousness.]
Siewart, Charles. *The Significance of Consciousness*. Princeton: Princeton University Press, 1998. [A balanced presentation of the place of consciousness in a culture dominated by science.]
Skribina, David. *Panpsychism in the West*. Cambridge: MIT Press, 2005. [A wonderful historical overview of the position that mind exists in some form in all living and nonliving things; this book stands in counterpoint to the scientific and materialist positions that now dominate the philosophy of mind.]
Sorabji, Richard. *Emotion and Peace of Mind*. New York: Oxford University Press, 2000.
———. *Self*. Chicago: University of Chicago Press, 2006. [A superb historical examination of individuality, life, and death.]
Suzuki, Daisetz Teitaro. *Mysticism: Christian and Buddhist*. New York: Dover, 2002. [The classic presentation of comparative mysticism.]
Swinburne, Richard. *The Evolution of the Soul*. Revised Edition. New York: Oxford University Press, 1997. [A dualistic interaction argument for the evolution of the soul.]
Vaught, Carl. *Access to God in Augustine's Confessions. Books X–XIII*. Albany State University of New York Press, 2005. [Third volume of this classic study.]
———. *Encounters with God in Augustine's Confessions. Books VII–IX*. Albany: State University of New York Press, 2004. [Second volume of this remarkable study.]

———. *The Journey toward God in Augustine's Confessions. Books I–VI.* Albany: State University of New York Press, 2003. [The first part of a masterful account of Augustine's spiritual journey.]

Wallace, B. Alan. *Mind in the Balance.* New York: Columbia University Press, 2009. [This book explores the place of meditation in science, Buddhism, and Christianity.]

———. *The Taboo of Subjectivity.* New York: Oxford University Press, 2000. [A demanding argument against the presuppositions of materialism.]

Weber, Michel, and Anderson Weekes. editors, *Process Approaches to Consciousness in Psychology, Neuroscience and Philosophy of Mind* (Albany: State University of New York Press, 2009. [Without a doubt the most advanced collection of essays bearing on the importance of process philosophy for consciousness studies]

Weissman, David. *Lost Souls.* Albany: State University of New York Press, 2003. [A clear, concise presentation of the philosophical mistakes that have landed us in our present cultural dilemma.]

Whitehead, Alfred North. *Adventures of Ideas.* New York: The Free Press, 1967.

———. *Modes of Thought.* New York: Free, 1968.

———. *Process and Reality.* Corrected Edition. Edited by Griffin and Sherburne. New York: The Free Press, 1978.

———. *Science and the Modern World.* New York: Free, 1967. [All four books comprise the foundation of Whitehead's philosophy of organism that in my judgment is the most powerful alternative to the materialism that now dominates the philosophy of mind.]

Wiebe, Phillip. *God and Other Spirits.* New York: Oxford University Press, 2004. [Exploring Christianity's "intimations" of transcendence.]

Wienpahl, Paul. *The Radical Spinoza.* New York: New York University Press, 1979. [A radical reinterpretation of Spinoza that demonstrates his close connection to Zen Buddhism.]

Zimmer, Carl. *Soul Made Flesh.* New York: Free Press, 2004. [The history of the discovery of the brain and its impact on the world.]

INDEX

Allan, George, xii
Ames, Roger, xii

Beck, Aaron, 14, 111–13
Bhante Gunaratana Henepola, 14, 111–13
Buddhism, 2, 7, 80, 94–96, 109, 112–15

Cobb, John, xii
Code, Murray, 65
Cognitive Therapy, 14, 113–15
Confucius (and Confucianism), 2, 9, 60, 99, 115
Consciousness, 10–11, 17–19, 41 ff., 95
Contrast, 9 and passim
Cosmology, ix–x, 4–5, 48
Creativity, 18–19 and passim

Dao, *see* Taoist
Dylan, Bob, 31, 47–49

Eloquence, 9–10, 11–12
  Eloquence Arising, 53–67
Epilogue, 117
Eternal and Temporal Contrasts, 4, 12–13, 69–83, 95–102, 110

Factor of the Integer, 10, 20–22, 38, 118
fallacy of misplaced concreteness, xi, 2, 28, 38, 98

Feeling The Alternatives, 10, 13, 19, 29–30, 38, 41–67, 74, 95–98, 114
Felt Intelligence, 9 and ff., 23 and ff., 31, 33, 48–49, 96, 100, 116
Form, 17 and passim
Four Orders of Feelings, 28 ff., 54

Grange, Claudine, 133
  Cognitive Therapist
Griffin, David Ray, xii
Grossman, Neal, 13, 92, 121

Haecceitas, 16–18, 21–24
Hall, David, xii
Harmony, 9 and passim
Healing the Mind, 13 and passim
Heraclitus, 1, 7
Hermana Juanita de las Hermanas de San Geronimo, 25
Hinduism, 2, 4, 20
Hopkins, Gerard Manley, 15–18, 23, 119
Horney, Karen, 65

Imagination, 43–46, 49, 64 ff., 87 ff.
Inscape, 9, 15 and passim
Integration and Transformation, 17–25 and passim
Intensity of feeling, 18 and passim
Involvement, 27 and passim

John of the Cross, ix, 25
Joyce, James, 69
   Theory of Beauty, 117 ff.
   Ulysses, 55

Knowledge and Action, 35–37

Langer, Susanne, 10, 20–22, 38, 74 ff.
Limitation and Value, 62 ff.

Mysticism, xii, 73, 92–95, 110–11
   Masked, Practical Mystics, 85, 117–18

Neville, Robert, xii, 12, 19–20, 69–75, 83–84, 118–19, 121
New Axial Age, 115–16

Peirce, C. S., 11, 54 ff.
   Postscript, 121
   semiotics, 102 ff.
Process, 17–21, 32 ff., 42 ff., 64 ff., 98–100

Realm of Meaning, 63–67
Rilke, Rainer Maria, 10, 31, 39

The Sign of Diversion, 104–109
The Sign of Mindfulness, 110–14
Signs of the Times, 101–16
Slave 'Hoot,' 7–8, 23, 29, 49, 58
Soul
   as colloquial term, 8–9
   as dead or alive, 66, 121
   as expression, x and passim
   healing of, 82–84
   Reclamation, 1–8
   Soul making, 121
   as in soul work, 85–100
Spinoza
   concept of God, 86 ff.
   emotions, 75–92
   eternity, 75–84
   intellectual love of God, 82–84
   metaphysics of identity, 97–98
   method of Soul Work, 88–94
   three ways of knowing, 78–81
Subjectivity, 17 and passim

Tao Te Ching, 60, 73 ff., 120
Taoist, 2, 7, 16, 18, 20, 45, 48, 60, 99, 115
Trilogy of *Nature, The City, Soul*, ix, 4–5, 116, 119
Truth, 34 and passim
Truthful Beauty, 8, 11 ff., 44, 60 ff.

Vipassana (Insight) Meditation, 14, 111–15

Wang Yang-ming, 13, 35–37, 96, 118
Wartofsky, Marx, 97
Weissman, David, xii
Whitehead, Alfred North, ix and passim
   See also Truthful Beauty

Xin, Heartmind, 2, 9, 36, 62

Zen, 2, 45, 47, 62

www.ingramcontent.com/pod-product-compliance
Lightning Source LLC
Chambersburg PA
CBHW021145230426
43667CB00005B/256